On All Sides Nowhere

On All Sides
NOWHERE

BUILDING
A LIFE IN RURAL
IDAHO

William Gruber

A MARINER ORIGINAL
Houghton Mifflin Company
Boston • *New York*
2002

For information about permission to reproduce selections from
this book, write to Permissions, Houghton Mifflin Company,
215 Park Avenue South, New York, New York 10003.

Visit our Web site: www.houghtonmifflinbooks.com.

Library of Congress Cataloging-in-Publication Data is available.

ISBN 0-618-18929-7

Printed in the United States of America

Book design by Robert Overholtzer

QUM 10 9 8 7 6 5 4 3 2 1

The author is grateful for permission to reprint "Hay for the
Horses," from *Riprap* and *Cold Mountain Poems* by Gary Snyder.
Copyright © 1990 by Gary Snyder. Reprinted by permission of
North Point Press, a division of Farrar, Straus and Giroux, LLC.

AUTHOR'S NOTE
The events depicted in this book are true to the best of my
recollection. I have changed the names of some of the
people to protect their privacy.

This book is for Nancy,
everywhere in these pages

From nowhere. On all sides nowhere.

—Samuel Beckett, *A Piece of Monologue*

CONTENTS

BREAD LOAF AND
THE BAKELESS PRIZES

SINCE 1926 the Bread Loaf Writers' Conference has convened every August in the shadow of Bread Loaf Mountain in Vermont's Green Mountains, where Middlebury College maintains a summer campus. The conference, founded by Robert Frost and Willa Cather — a generation before creative writing became a popular course of study — brings together established poets and prose writers, editors, and literary agents to work with writers at various stages of their careers. Frost's plan for the conference included a faculty of distinguished writers who would "turn from correcting grammar in red ink to matching experience in black ink, experience of life and experience of art." Bread Loaf has stayed true to Frost's original vision, and its vibrancy and energy have helped make it the most respected of the many summer writers' conferences in the nation.

While part of Bread Loaf's reputation was built on the writers associated with it — W. H. Auden, Sinclair Lewis, Wallace Stegner, Katherine Anne Porter, William Carlos Williams, Ralph Ellison, Nelson Algren, Toni Morrison, Adrienne Rich, May Sarton, Archibald MacLeish, Frank O'Connor, and Richard Wright, among others — it has an equally high reputation for finding and supporting writers of promise at the earliest stages of their careers. Eudora Welty, Carson McCullers, Anne Sexton, May Swenson, Russell Banks, Joan Didion, Miller Williams, Richard Yates,

Richard Ford, Julia Alvarez, Carolyn Forché, Linda Pastan, Dave Smith, Tess Gallagher, Ellen Bryant Voigt, Andrea Barrett, and Tim O'Brien are some of the poets, novelists, and short story writers who benefited from the scholarships and fellowships Bread Loaf awards annually.

The importance of Bread Loaf for American writers is typified by Julia Alvarez's recollection of her first conference: "I went to Bread Loaf for the first time in 1969 and fell in love with the community of writers . . . All these people talking about nothing but writing, forcing me to think about writing! I aspired to this great society." My own relationship with Bread Loaf began in 1981 when I attended as a scholar, and was renewed in 1986 when I returned as a fellow. These initial opportunities allowed me to work with William Stafford and Philip Levine, whose influence helped to shape the way I think of myself as a writer. Later, as an associate faculty member and since 1995 as director, I have repeatedly witnessed the profound effect the eleven days in August have on those who attend. John Ciardi, a former director of the conference and one of its most eloquent spokespeople, liked to say about the Bread Loaf experience that "no great writer ever became one in isolation. Somewhere and sometime, if only at the beginning, he had to experience the excitement and intellectual ferment of a group something like this."

There are many obstacles to a successful literary career, but none is more difficult to overcome than the publication of a first book. The Katharine Bakeless Nason Literary Publication Prizes were established in 1995 to expand Bread Loaf's commitment to the support of emerging writers. Endowed by the LZ Francis Foundation, whose directors wished to commemorate Middlebury College patron Katharine Bakeless Nason and to encourage emerging writers, the Bakeless Prizes launch the publication career of a poet, fiction writer, and creative nonfiction writer annually. Winning manuscripts are chosen in an open, national competition by a distinguished judge in each genre. The winning books are published in August to coincide with the Bread Loaf Writers' Conference, and the authors are invited to participate as Bakeless Fellows.

Since they first appeared in 1996, the winning Bakeless books have been critical successes. As a result, the Bakeless Prizes are coveted among new writers. The fact that Houghton Mifflin publishes these books is significant, for it joins together one of America's oldest and most distinguished literary presses with an equally distinguished writers' conference. The collaboration speaks to the commitment of both institutions to cultivate emerging literary artists in order to ensure a richer future for American writing.

MICHAEL COLLIER
Director, Bread Loaf Writers' Conference

FOREWORD

THERE HAS always been a lot of claptrap written about American rural life. Piety, kitsch, self-importance, sentimentalism — these deadly literary sins seem to thrive on good clean country air. Even Thoreau, flinty contrarian and poet laureate of bucolic solitude, packed a full load of pomposity into *Walden*. It is a subtle and demanding trick, apparently, to write about wilderness and backwoods folk in a fresh, uncondescending way. William Gruber manages it neatly in this book, finding a combination of elegy, erudition, passion, Namib-dry humor, self-deprecation, and long reflection that serves, in the end, to carry us deep into the life of an unusually remote American place. Having a sackful of good stories and characters to draw from doesn't hurt his cause.

Gruber and his young wife bought and moved onto forty acres (with abandoned log cabin) in the wooded back blocks of the Idaho panhandle in the early seventies, just when a lot of other young Americans (*Walden* in back pockets) were doing something similar. But Gruber makes very little of this ambient social movement beyond noting its peculiar refraction through the resolutely local lens of longtime Alder Creek residents, who see alien "hippies" only on TV. He is impressively selective as he chooses what to tell and what to elide. The births of his children, the construction of his house, the quotable mutterings, undoubtedly amusing, of his formidable wife — all of these occur offstage. This is not a soul-baring family memoir, though it is largely about a family's life and it does bare its share of soul.

The book has the texture of affectionate inquiry. The author moves to an obscure, climatically unforgiving corner of the country braced for solitude, deprivation, self-reliance. Instead, he finds himself becoming a member of an intimate (if far-flung), impoverished (but socially rich) mutual-aid society whose rituals and denizens and native arts invite (and reward) long-term apprenticeship and investigation. Just asking an elderly neighbor for advice about whether to buy the forty acres becomes a lesson in land-reading, in the defining importance of water in the West, and in the fine local style of wryness. Gruber learns, of necessity, to fell trees, and the dangers, pleasures, and complexity of low-tech logging come sharply into focus. Essays on the chainsaw and the peculiar language of sawyers follow naturally. Something you may be curious about — how much land *is* forty acres, anyway? — gets studied and described from various angles until you feel you know as much about the subject as you will ever know from reading.

Speaking of reading, Gruber was a graduate student when he lived in Idaho (he is now a professor in Georgia), and a large part of this book is, in unexpected ways, about learning how to read. "Living in Alder Creek opened my eyes to the essential realism of great writers," he claims, and the claim feels justified, for he embeds his observations in resonant literary and historical contexts and carefully sketches neighbors who could have stepped from the pages of Samuel Beckett or John Berger. Indeed, Gruber's treatment of his neighbors may be the most striking and sophisticated aspect of this memoir. It's easy enough, inferring from the social cues, to see that most of the people in Alder Creek, whether new arrivals or the descendants of homesteaders, occupy modest positions on the American status ladder, as that structure is usually understood. But Gruber's understanding is not usual. He offers no statistics on poverty, education, income, or unwed motherhood for his "underprivileged" community. Rather, he takes the place on its own terms, honoring the ingenuity and expertise of the people he admires, while letting the hardship and despair — the failure, suicides, and madness, the terrible transiency of many of the people who wash up in such a backwater — fill what seem to be their rightful share of the picture. Specificity is his most powerful tool. The communal life he celebrates never feels prettified. There are no barn-raisings or old-time hoedowns, just endless unfinished "build-ons" (home improvement projects, usually quixotic or hideous or both) and sudden giddy gatherings to scavenge grain spilled in a train derailment.

The odd, almost timeless, intensely insular life depicted here intersects at one point with events in the greater world. For generations, and during the first years Gruber lived there, people in Alder Creek had been helping themselves to what is known as "dead and down" timber on the land around them. Legally, of course, the wood belonged to the land's owners — railroads, timber companies, various absentees, the federal government — and yet custom had created a local "right" to collect a reasonable amount of fallen timber for personal use. Gruber traces this practice to "a principle first enunciated in the Anglo-Saxon codes of medieval England: to the peasant belonged the windfalls." He gets a kick out of this connection, and out of this practice, and comparing himself and his neighbors to peasants, which he does elsewhere as well, is in no sense forelock-tugging. (Like John Berger, he obviously finds peasants more interesting than he does most modern folk.) Then comes the world energy crisis of 1975, a huge spike in the popularity of wood heat in America, an invasion of Alder Creek by serious woodcutters with serious rigs, the swift disappearance from local forests of dead and down timber, a new legal attitude on the part of the timber corporations — and the end of a way of life for the neo-peasants in that part of Idaho. It's a queer, poignant episode, recalled with strong feeling but without sentimentality. Rural life in America is, in Gruber's scrupulous version, both a premodern idyll and a tough, very particular, battered, beloved place.

WILLIAM FINNEGAN

PREFACE

IT IS IMPOSSIBLE to explain the circumstances of this book without explaining what brought me to Idaho in the first place. I moved to the panhandle of Idaho in the summer of 1972, newly married and without any visible means of support. More than a year before that I had abandoned a career in journalism. The immediate reason for quitting my job reporting the news for the *Melbourne Age* was boredom. The decisive event was the day when, having spent five long weeks covering a naval court of inquiry into the sinking of an Australian coastal steamer, I learned that, in the official opinion of the board, the *Noongah* had sunk, *mirabile dictu,* "because of an excessive ingress of water." The deeper cause for leaving journalism, however, was ethical. After nearly two years as a journalist I had covered my share of hijackings, murders, and wrecks of one kind or another, and I could no longer bear to interview people deep in shock or grief. I came to doubt that I had any real business making money by publicizing misfortune. Writing fiction seemed a more honest trade.

But in the course of many ensuing months I had not exactly managed to win fame and fortune peddling fiction to little magazines, and it was clear even in the early seventies in America, a time when "dropping out" was a perfectly legitimate way of life, that I had to do *something.* Maybe it's true, as George Bernard Shaw is supposed to have said: Those who can, do; those who can't, teach. So I applied to graduate schools in some of the most remote places in the contiguous forty-eight states, collected the forms for veterans' education benefits, and started to assemble the clothes and tools I thought would be useful for country life. One of the places that accepted me was the University of Idaho in Moscow; at the time, I'm embarrassed to confess, its chief attraction was that it seemed to be located farther than any other university from interstate highways. The plan was to attend graduate school in English, teaching at the same time to earn a modest income and still trying to write. I planned at first to stay in Idaho beyond the time it took to earn a graduate degree, although the plans of a twenty-something to "stay" somewhere don't mean much. I guess it would be more accurate to say that when my wife and I moved to Idaho we had not thought our lives through to the point where we imagined moving again. The two years it would take to complete a program of study seemed at that time to stretch well beyond the foreseeable horizon.

The original motive for moving to the panhandle of Idaho was partly political, partly selfish. I was weary of the hypocrisy of Nixon's America and the alarming dissolution of urban civilization, and I wanted to disconnect myself from city surroundings and bury myself in books — the ones I planned to read, the ones I hoped to write. I would go back to the land and back to school at the same time. In my mind's eye, I saw myself as a successor to Edward Abbey, to Thoreau, to Hesiod. In the eyes of most of the people who knew me, what I was doing was a lot less respectable. My father-in-law, for one, took a dim view of the whole enterprise — as I guess most fathers-in-law take a dim view of their daughter's husband's prospects. He was worried, as I discovered years later, that living in rural north Idaho we would "lose our edge."

One thing led to another, and we stayed in Idaho not only for the two years it took me to finish a master's degree in English at the University of Idaho in Moscow but also for the four more years it took to complete a Ph.D. at Washington State University, just over the state line in nearby Pullman. We did not live in town. Our search for a place to live in the country took us farther and farther afield until we wound up buying an abandoned log cabin and forty acres of broken meadow and second-growth timber about fifty miles north of the university. The mailing address was

St. Maries, but the postal version of our whereabouts was seriously misleading. The town itself lay more than twenty road miles from our place, which was located in an area sparsely settled even for Idaho. Locals knew it as Alder Creek.

It made for a prodigious commute, although I usually drove it in just over an hour, even in the snow — not bad at all by modern suburban standards. I doubt if I could have kept my sanity and marriage together if I had tried it on a nine-to-five schedule, but the flexible hours of a graduate student made the arrangement feasible, and so for almost seven years I lived a life about equally divided between town and country, between Restoration drama, poststructuralism, and teaching freshman composition on the one hand, and, on the other, wood heat, livestock, and perennially broken plumbing. The two orders of being were impossibly unrelated, and so together they made for a wonderfully satisfying life. By the time we left Alder Creek the land was bought and paid for, we had made dozens of close friends, and it just seemed right that, whatever the vagaries of fortune, we would hang on to that place as a kind of home.

What I thought I wanted from Idaho was something similar to what Thoreau found on the banks of Walden Pond: simplicity, economy, and ascetic isolation from the press of human culture. But instead of finding the solitude and cerebration I thought I wanted, life in Alder Creek shook me up. Instead of isolation, I found community; instead of rural stolidity, I found intelligence and wisdom, more than enough to correct my foolish ideas about books and about education. Life there proved to be splendidly energetic, rich in thought and in society. To call Alder Creek small is an error, a failing of head and heart.

I wrote this book to honor that place and the people who lived there. The essays that follow have an overlapping chronology; the highest art I could achieve would be the art of the historian. But part of my graduate education — perhaps the most important part — was discovering the intersections of life and literature, and a history without the detours and digressions of romance would be incomplete. The book is a collection of personal essays about one small part of Idaho, and it is also unashamedly a love song.

Georgia O'Keeffe, upon first seeing the American West (she was talking in particular about New Mexico), claimed, "From then on, I was always on my way back."

Me too. I moved away from Alder Creek in August of 1979, though most summers I contrive to make my way back to that place. Like Antaeus, I've got to keep in touch. As for the places since then, they all seem hitched on, somehow lacking in substance and authenticity. Anywhere else, no matter how long the sojourn, I've been there unconvinced and unbelieving. If you ask me, I'll say that I've been there only on assignment.

On All Sides Nowhere

IDAHO FIRST REGISTERED on my consciousness at the movies. In the summer of 1960 I was sixteen, and in the middle of August there was no place in suburban Pennsylvania to find air conditioning except in supermarkets or theaters. I could not spend summer days amid the cabbages and canned goods, and so to escape the heat I went with my friends as often as I could to the movies; one of the movies I sought out was an elegy for the waning days of modern civilization, *On the Beach*.

To the filmgoing public in 1960, keenly aware that despite all the best intentions the cold war could suddenly turn hot, the movie was perfectly credible. It was set only a few years into the future; a calendar on the wall read, ominously, "1964." Nuclear war of undisclosed origins had killed everyone in the Northern Hemisphere, and now, as a lethal cloud of radiation spread slowly over the planet, one of the last surviving groups of humans clustered in Melbourne, Australia, to await the end. It was an intoxicating, almost carnivalesque, experience. Gregory Peck played the romantic lead opposite Ava Gardner, and at one point in the film, Peck, the taciturn commander of a nuclear submarine, tells Ava Gardner about his origins. In answer to her question about his childhood home, he replies with a single word that at the time seemed more homiletic than informative: "Idaho."

Whose decision was it for Peck to claim Idaho for his birthplace? Of all the possible states the scriptwriter could have chosen, why that one? And it *was* a choice: for the record, Peck was born in La Jolla, California, and his character in Nevil Shute's novel from which the movie was adapted comes from Westport, Connecticut. Peck's "Idaho" drops like a stone into a well of unknown depth; it falls without trace, without echo. It is a piece, apparently, of purely gratuitous information.

Why Idaho? The name resonates oddly with Melbourne and San Francisco, the environments of *On the Beach*. Those places set the mood of the film. To Americans in 1960, Melbourne was alien, exotic, and San Francisco brought to mind the glitz and romance of California. Set in that context, and set against the despairing hedonism of humans who number their remaining days according to the drifting global winds, "Idaho" seems dissonant. Its sound is stark, but as Peck speaks it, it sounds also moral and attractive. It seems to express Peck's loneliness, his longing for the simplicity of childhood and for the innocence of a world before the Bomb. None of the familiar mythic names of the American West, not Texas or Oregon or Colorado, would have the same aura of pure expressivity. My guess is that the name "Idaho" was chosen for its semantic emptiness. The name made sense because to most people "Idaho" meant nothing, and, meaning nothing, it could stand in for the infinite pathos of a world that would shortly cease to exist. Idaho was then, and in some ways still is, a geographic *What You Will*, and as a result the name "Idaho" becomes a kind of cultural Rorschach test for whoever happens to reflect on it.

A road map of Idaho, if you focus on the narrow strip of land that sits atop the main bulge of the state, will show U.S. 95 extending upward from the town of Lewiston on the Snake River and running due north until it touches British Columbia. U.S. 95 is the only north–south road in the state; for most of its five hundred–odd miles, its major function is commercial. On it, apart from a few weeks in summer at the height of the vacation season, wheat and wood chips move south to the granaries in Moscow or the pulp mills in Lewiston, logs by the tens of thousands head north to the lake towns of Coeur d'Alene, Post Falls, and Sandpoint. On that map, halfway between Moscow and

Coeur d'Alene, several miles above a couple of minuscule settlements designated, echoically, Desmet and Tensed, a thin blue line splits off from U.S. 95 and runs due east for twenty miles until it dead-ends in Idaho 5 coming north from St. Maries.

Nothing much shows on that road big enough to be named; it starts from nowhere, goes to noplace. Travelers on it turn their backs on the rolling grainlands of eastern Washington and head toward a low wall of mountains, smooth, rounded, thick with timber. The change in topography is instantaneous. In less than two miles they're in the foothills of the Bitterroots, the westernmost range of the Rocky Mountains, scarcely seventy-five miles from the Montana border. Once over the first row of hills, the road descends again and presses deeper into those foothills for fifteen miles or so, following alongside the Benewah Creek and through the Benewah Valley.

Houses and landmarks on that road are few. It's a gravel road, in theory at least, but for much of its length it's better described as a dirt road backed up with whatever rocks nature or the Benewah County road crew found time to strew there. "I lived here better than twenty years," the owner of Benewah Motors, Wally Krassalt, once told me as we made our way from town out toward my place to diagnose my ailing Land Rover, "and I never once saw the Benewah Road in good shape."

Much of the time the road follows alongside the Benewah Creek, running slightly above the creek through draws filled with alder and aspen or traversing occasional flatlands and pockets of deep forest. You drive along the road with no real sense of progress. It's hard to mark the miles: there are no towns to encounter, no height toward which to aspire, just a succession of curves and glimpses of fields and pockets of forest so similar that they are valueless as landmarks. If you pursue the Benewah Road almost to its terminus at State 5, you come upon a Dumpster, angle-parked on a turnout on the downhill side of the road, positioned so that as you discard your trash you can look out and down at a postcard view of the southernmost end of a chain of glacial lakes that stretch from St. Maries north almost to Canada. On most days the Dumpster overflows with abandoned household goods, broken bedsteads and electrical components, scraps of carpet, Sheetrock, and lumber, random tools or parts of tools, bald and shredded tires, and pieces of cars. At one time some local wag took a can of bright orange paint and sprayed "Benewah Shop-n-Save" on the side of the Dumpster. Like all good humor, it had one foot in reality; my neighbors and I checked that Dumpster regularly, like a lottery ticket.

Long before you encounter the Dumpster, though, if you are headed east from U.S. 95, you pass a spot marked on your map as "Benewah." Maps denote "Benewah" with a small blue circle, as if to promise travelers a settlement of some kind or other situated about midway along the road, but the maps promise more than ever existed. Even in the heyday of north Idaho logging and homesteading, there never was a town named Benewah. The place is recognizable as a civic location only because of two buildings, an abandoned one-room school, painted, the time I first saw it, bright pink, and a swaybacked frame structure with a faded sign, "Benewah General Store," and because of a smaller dirt road that dead-ends at the Benewah Road just east of the schoolhouse. Less than a hundred yards along that lesser road a sign cautions you that there should be "No Heavy Hauling When Surface Is Soft." In one instant, if you read it attentively, that sign tells you much about the local climate and economy as well as the politics and favorite pastimes of the people who live there. The sign, like every other sign the county erected along that road, is riddled with small holes; it's an instance either of vandalism or of "bullet art," depending on your point of view. As you pass by the sign, the road begins to climb out of the valley and heads into the timber. Now you're on the road to Alder Creek.

We bought forty acres of land, about the smallest amount of land available then by way of rural subdivision. Our forty acres were a quarter part of the 160 acres that had once belonged to a family named Deja. In the early decades of the twentieth century the place was the headquarters for a local logging crew, and then, the timber gone and the land valueless to the company that owned it, the land passed as a second-generation homestead to Deja. Our place contained Deja's house, a log cabin about twenty by thirty feet with green cardboard interior walls and two antiquated but functioning wood stoves, a ruinous and older cabin that had been built in 1915 as a bunkhouse for a crew of loggers, and a lovely and graceful barn with the top half of its roof missing. Around the house were two, maybe three acres of meadow and pasture dotted with huge stumps left from the first time that particular piece of land had ever lost trees to human hands. Most of them were burned black, evidence of someone's vain attempt to turn cutover timberland into pasture. The rest of our place, officially 37.5 acres according to the tax records, was woodland.

Forty acres is a big place to someone used to measuring his horizons in terms of city blocks, although I soon understood that a square of land one-quarter mile on a side was much too insignificant to register against the immensity of the American West. Translated into its legal description, our forty acres seemed downright puny: we owned merely the northeast quarter of the northeast quarter of Section 32, Township 45 North, Range 3 West, Boise Meridian. That legal description reflects the surveyor's grid that was laid down over the western half of the country when it was opened for development. Homesteads were designated as one quarter of a section, or 160 acres — more than large enough to make a living if the land was fertile and the growing season long, but in northern Idaho too small to do much other than to cut the timber and sell out. The real winners in the development of much of the American West were not the homesteaders but the railroads, which, in exchange for their efforts and expenses at laying track, were granted alternating sections of land along their rights of way. A mile of track, 640 acres of land: it made for estates the size of which would have put a dukedom to shame, and it made the railroads rich. Even in the 1970s, when the railroads nationally were losing money by carloads, the Burlington Northern compensated for its losses by selling timber from its vast holdings.

Before Deja owned it, our place had been the site of a logging camp. The original bunkhouse was situated by the road, and we found rusty sections of rail and rail spikes in the grass by the barn, the remnants of a small logging railroad that had been built down the draw of our creek to where it debouched into a bigger stream that fed the main fork of Alder Creek. To the north across the road lay two of the three remaining forties from the Deja place, owned then by absentees, and about a mile to the east was the Brede ranch house, unoccupied except during the summer grazing season and fall roundup. Beyond us to the south was a large, lightly timbered meadow, almost a savannah, and beyond that lay a mile or more of dense forest that ended at the Alder Creek Loop Road. Our closest neighbors lived along that road: Ed and Jean Strobel, Jim Yearout, Bud and Bertha Yearout, and "Cotton" and Peggy Stanridge. With the exception of the Strobels, they had all lived in Alder Creek for decades.

The first days on our farm were full of emptiness; I had never known such quiet, and with the stillness came many unexpected discoveries. Sitting high atop the barn roof one afternoon I heard for the first time the rush of air over a crow's wings as it flew by overhead. Mornings in the cold, still air you could sometimes pick up traces of conversation spoken nearly half a mile away at the Brede ranch, and later in the winter I often stood on the porch simply to listen to the falling snow. It fell with a hiss, the lightness of which buoyed the spirits like a sleeping child's breath.

Our place hardly resembled Laura Ingalls Wilder's "little house in the big woods." On three sides of our land lay the open rangeland of the Brede ranch, and on the remaining northern side meandered the county road. So we could not think of ourselves as living on the edge of a forest, much less a wilderness. But still it gave us pleasure to contemplate owning a woods big enough to get lost in for a short time, if only you remembered not to walk too long in a straight line, and big enough too to support its own wildlife population. We had our own resident deer, coyotes, grouse, and beavers. In the meadows wildflowers grew in great profusion: dandelions, lupine, and wild roses in May; ox-eye daisies, Indian paintbrush, and mustard in summer; and Canada thistles in late August, on those days when you felt the first chill of fall in the morning air.

And we had mushrooms. One of our entertainments in April and early May was to hunt wild mushrooms, mainly morels. One day, not long after we were living in our cabin, Nancy came across several women with baskets tramping through the woods. They were members of the Spokane Mushroom Club, they said, and they had hunted morels on this land for years. Despite her assurances that they were still welcome to hunt our land, we never saw them again. But their visit was the inspiration for our own interest in hunting mushrooms, and each year during the early spring there was nothing more important to us than gathering morels.

Part of the reason we hunted mushrooms was economic; we were always looking for ways to stretch our budget. But the economic value of twenty pounds of morel mushrooms — a good annual harvest — was insignificant in relation to the social value of the hunt. Hunting mushrooms and talking about hunting mushrooms were communal enterprises for us and for our neighbors, almost a cult; the sociability of the activity increased its satisfaction. Nancy became the expert, and she recruited our daughter Elaine as soon as she could walk; together they endured cold, rain, snow, and gloom as they made the rounds of their favorite, often secret glades.

Some of the appeal of foraging in the woods was the experience, new for us, of being in tune with the natural world. Hunting mushrooms, you focused on the smallest of environmental details, the texture and color of scales on a fallen cone (these closely resembled young morels) or the contours of the forest duff (small mushrooms, especially young boletes, often lay partly hidden under a carpet of needles). And some of the attraction was distinctly sensual. Sure, the morel vaguely resembles a phallus, but this erotic shape wasn't really part of their emotional and intellectual appeal. Mushrooms have always been symbols of potent unconscious forces, forces as potentially dangerous as they are liberating, and so one of their charms comes from the knowledge that unlike, say, corn or asparagus, wild mushrooms are not entirely under human control. At times, hunting mushrooms became a mystical experience; as the author of one field guide puts it, hunting mushrooms is "not simply a matter of traipsing through the woods in winter. It is an art, a skill, a meditation, and a process."

Driving across the country I still play the childhood game of looking for rare license plates. Of all the states, none appears more seldom than Idaho. I've seen plates from Alaska and even Hawaii more often than from Idaho; it's as if something about the environment breeds people who stay close to home. "There is no stranger destination," writes Marilynne Robinson, than Idaho, "nor odder origin." Each year people ask me where I spend the summer. I say "Idaho," and I can tell by the emptiness of their faces that my answer put them in a state of social uneasiness. To tell an easterner you're planning a trip to Idaho is to strain the rules of etiquette. There's never a comfortable response. It goes beyond mere puzzlement. Sometimes I can see them weighing what they know about me against what they have heard on television about separatist movements or Aryan Nation. Then, in an effort to fill the awkward silence, they ask whether I have relatives in northern Idaho, or they make a joke about potatoes. Other times they misconstrue Idaho for Iowa. This happens more often than you would think possible, and then they tell me about their cousin in Des Moines or the time they drove with their kids through the Midwest. Or sometimes they just look at me with a genial inquisitorial stare, the way you imagine Jane Goodall contemplating the behavior of a mountain ape.

Even in an age when everybody is wired to everybody and everything else, Idaho remains elusive. The name itself is a trap for the unwary. "Idaho," according to widespread myth, comes from Native American dialect, "Ee-da-how." This means, I was taught as a child, "light on the mountain" or "the sun comes down the mountain." Truth is, that story, like the story about Eskimos having dozens of separate words for "snow," is fiction. The Inuit have no more than the usual number of words that occur in most Indo-European languages to refer to the different varieties of frozen precipitation, and "Idaho" doesn't approximate any known

Native American word. It doesn't mean what we think it means. In fact, it probably doesn't mean anything at all. It's most likely a coined word, a polysyllabic assembly made up a long time ago by some unknown promoter who wanted a name that would sound romantic to a population who dreamed of striking it rich in the West. "Idaho" is to the states of America as "Häagen-Dazs" is to brands of ice cream. Both names are empty, meaningless sets of sounds invented to impress a gullible public. In this way it mimics the history of much of the West. When, in 1803, on the eve of the sale of the vast amount of land that was then called simply Louisiana, Napoleon was asked by his minister Talleyrand exactly what he should tell the Americans they were about to purchase, the emperor responded, "If an obscurity did not already exist, it would perhaps be good policy to put one there." Talleyrand obediently reported to the Americans that they should "construe it [Louisiana] in their own way."

If Idaho is hard to fix in the mind, it's even harder to come to a clear opinion about it. Much of the popular press about Idaho isn't good. Dave Barry in his columns regularly makes fun of it, and in the minds of a hundred million Americans right now, Idaho is the place where Richard Butler located his national socialist church, and it's the place to which Mark Fuhrman retired after being disgraced during the trial of O. J. Simpson.

My experience of north Idaho is different. What sets Idaho apart is not its atavism but its openness to change and to difference. If I had to sum up its ethos I would say this: it's a place where an amazing tolerance extends to every person. In Idaho, your background doesn't count for a whole lot; here you're liked or not depending on what you say and do starting from the time you arrive. Many times in the days when I had a beard I met with longtime residents of Benewah County who professed to dislike "hippies," which to them apparently meant anyone alien, young, and hairy. Yet in spite of the fact that I looked like the sort of person their televisions had taught them to be afraid of, I was always welcomed warmly into their houses. They talked to me, they sometimes fed me, and they always gave me their best advice. For the locals, hippies were always somebody other than the person they were talking to.

In many ways, it's the place where time stopped, where you can find, as Montanans like to advertise about themselves, the last best place. But much of what is good about the state results not from its spectacular geography but from its emptiness. People are still relatively few in number in Idaho, and apart from Boise there's nothing that can claim the title "city." In 1990, the census counted barely half of the state's population as living in towns with populations greater than 2,500. Idaho is still isolated ranches and small towns, and with those towns and ranches comes a hunger for companionship and a belief that simple human contact is the pearl beyond price. I still remember the day in 1974 I received by mail a license plate for my truck. This was in the days before private citizens could choose to lower their plate numbers in inverse relationship to the size of their individual ego. The number on my plate was unbelievable: 67.

That number was a constant reminder of the relative sparsity of humans in Idaho; all my neighbors had numbers like that. It made for an odd sight in parking lots and along side streets in St. Maries; the lineup of license plates made me think I'd stumbled onto a convention of big shots: 50 was parked next to 35 next to 122. And in a way I had: since then, the closest I've come to something like it is the row of cars at Emory University Hospital in the spaces reserved for hospital administrators and chiefs of surgery (although their cars are a little more upscale than you'd have seen parked in front of the IGA in St. Maries). Those memorable numbers were an affirmation of their owners' place in the order of things. And with that affirmation of identity came social responsibility. Here was a place where people could not escape their neighbors, and so could not escape themselves.

Idaho remains stubbornly incomprehensible, all things to all people. In geography books and in popular literature, Idaho is potatoes, silver mining, and Sun Valley. It's one of the states that kids are most likely to stumble on in their geography bees. Its capital, Boise, is impossibly unmemorable because to a third-grade mind the name, a derivative of *bois* ("woods" in French), seems to be a mental dead end in a way that "Austin" or "Olympia" or "Tallahassee" is not. "All Boise names," writes Lalia Phipps Boone, "are transferred from the name given the river by French Canadian explorers and trappers for the great variety of trees growing along its banks. After traveling over many miles of arid land, they are said to have exclaimed, '*Les bois, les bois! Voyez les bois.*'" What schoolchild would know, or, knowing, care about an etymology as happenstance as that?

The state seems to have confused even the federal government. "For many years," writes Leonard J. Arrington in his massive *History of Idaho*, "the United States could not make up its mind about this large inland area." In a way, that's still true. Even on a map the state looks odd. Its shape is illogical, way too thin at the top and disproportionately fat at the bottom. It looks as if it's missing some pieces or ought all to belong to something else. In fact the land that now comprises Idaho did once belong to something else. "It was included," says Arrington, "in the British Northwest until 1820, when it became part of the Oregon Country. In 1848 it was recognized as a piece of Oregon Territory, and in 1853 the northern half was inserted in newly created Washington Territory. When Oregon became a state in 1859, the entire area and parts of western Wyoming and Montana were absorbed in Washington Territory. But in 1863, when the difficulties of transportation made it impossible to govern the region from Olympia, Idaho was declared a separate territory that included all of present-day Montana and nearly all of present-day Wyoming. Not until 1868 did Idaho Territory emerge with its present state boundaries."

Look for stability and you find none. Over the course of eons the state has undergone changes in topography from mountaintop to ocean floor, and its climate has varied from the vulcanism of the Eocene period to the successive glaciations of the Ice Age. In between fire and ice, for a few million years, Idaho was tropical. And before its climate was tropical, it was literally coastal. For something like 700 million years, from the end of Precambrian time until about the middle of the Cretaceous period 100 million years ago, the western edge of Idaho *was* the coast. Westward from Idaho's shores 800 million years ago there stretched the open ocean. Except for the miracle of plate tectonics, Boise might be beachfront.

But nothing is less secure than the earth we stand on, and for hundreds of millions of years during the late Paleozoic and Mesozoic eras, the lithospheric plates that carried the floor of the Pacific Ocean and the entire North American continent drifted together. In time the floor and the continent collided — if an engagement that occurs at the speed of two inches a year can be called a collision. Every year brought land masses in the Pacific closer to the coastline. They came nearer by a mile or so every thirty-two thousand years, hurtling toward each other pell-mell, geologically speaking, until eventually west mashed east with a momentum of a quadrillion tons. It must have been a hell of a sight for whatever eyes were around to see it when the islands that are now the Okanogan Highlands docked in or around what was to become the city of Lewiston.

That collision and others like it raised the Rocky Mountains, so that the state of Idaho now lies between those prodigious mountains and the Pacific Ocean. It's the first land you reach after struggling across the Continental Divide. You might think that the Americans spilling westward over the mountains would have followed the established pattern of frontier settlement, filling the country up from east to west, so that they would homestead first in Idaho, then in Washington, Oregon, and California. Not so: Idaho has the curious distinction of being the last of the contiguous American states to be visited by American explorers. Even though several states were more remote, Idaho was for some reason the last place the early discoverers got to see. Not until August 12, 1805, when Meriwether Lewis looked down and west from the Continental Divide at the summit of Lemhi Pass, was the land that was to become Idaho seen by Euro-American eyes. Lewis seems not to have been particularly impressed. His journal records his discovery of "immense ranges of high mountains still to the west of us with their tops partially covered in snow" — at that point, what else was new? — and, after reconnoitering the western slopes of the Divide for about three fourths of a mile, he turned around and went back. He and Clark subsequently crossed and recrossed Idaho on their way to and from the Pacific.

Lewis and Clark's encounter with Idaho provided the type for a good part of the rest of the century of western settlement. Idaho was the place you went through on your way to someplace else. Your only ambition was to get through or over it. Between 1830 and 1850 thousands of white settlers traversed the southern part of the state on their way to Oregon and California, but only those who had the misfortune to die in Idaho stayed there. Except for the Jesuit mission a few miles west of Coeur d'Alene, the trading posts, Fort Hall and Fort Boise, and "a mountain man or two," writes Arrington, "no white settlers lived in Idaho for any length of time until 1855." In contrast to much of the rest of the West, which underwent extensive settlement and "development" in the middle decades of the nineteenth century, Idaho retained its aboriginal cultures as the only real populations. Not until the discovery of gold during the 1860s did permanent settlers arrive in Idaho in significant numbers, and it was only because of the developing market for northwestern timber at the end of the century, when supplies from the great midwestern forests had begun to dwindle, that Idaho was considered a likely place to homestead.

That history got a late start in Idaho turned out to be an unexpected piece of personal good fortune. What in most other places in the world counts as history still lies in Idaho in living memories. When Nancy and I moved to Alder Creek in 1972, we moved to one of the last regions of the United States where it was possible to talk to some of the men and women who had homesteaded it. The St. Maries telephone directory was so small you could comfortably fit it — folded, no less — into your hip pocket. And most of the names in that directory were the family names of the first Europeans to settle in that part of the country not quite a century ago. Little has changed since then. Even now you can talk to a handful of those first settlers. Among my friends then were some of those people, people who were alive in the first decade of the twentieth century, some of the first Europeans to walk Idaho land, breathe Idaho air, piss in Idaho snow.

Sometimes in the summer I drive the gravel roads to what is left of the houses of the people I knew and pull to the side and sit for a while on the hood of the truck. Solitude and open spaces may be what we think we seek, but it is social life that nourishes us, helps us grow. "Contemplation of nature alone," says Henry Walter Bates, "is not sufficient to fill the human heart and mind." Nearly all of the people who were my friends and neighbors in the years I lived in Alder Creek are dead now or have moved away, but it is because of them that the seven years I lived in Idaho were half magical and yet more real than anything else I have ever seen or done.

Things That Came
with the Place

The Well. Snow still pocked the ground in the spring of 1971 when I came upon what was to become our place in Alder Creek. In the last few days before the owner and I closed the deal I was in a daze of sorts and unable to make a decision. After three weeks of nights sleeping in a car and days looking at real estate, I had lost most of my sense of proportion. I would have bought swampland in Arizona just to bring an end to my shopper's delirium. It was time, I knew, to get a second opinion. So I asked Dick Benge if he would look over a place I was thinking about buying up near St. Maries.

Dick Benge lived about two miles outside of Princeton, a small town on State Route 6 more than thirty miles south of Alder Creek. (The towns Harvard and Yale were in the vicinity, too; I learned later that they were part of a series of college names that had been bestowed hopefully at the turn of the last century on stops along the main line of the Washington, Idaho, and Montana Railroad. Like Princeton, Harvard had grown to full status as a town, but I was puzzled at the time that Yale for some reason had remained only a railroad siding.) I picked up Benge at his house and together we drove out to the cabin.

Benge was one of dozens of people I met that May while I was looking for a place to buy. I met people in their yards, in their shops, in their houses. Like everyone else in Idaho, Benge interrupted what he was doing and happily talked for half an hour or more to somebody he'd never seen before. He was almost eighty, retired after more than half a century of working in the woods. He lived with his wife, Mae, enormously fat and enormously generous; like her husband, she had spent a lifetime in the woods, in her case cooking for hundreds of people who really had woodchoppers' appetites.

Benge and I stood in front of the cabin and looked out across the meadow to the barn and the trees, and I asked him what he thought. He didn't say anything at first. He looked around a bit and then walked through the grass to a tarpaper shed near the fence. He didn't seem much interested in the house; having lived in north Idaho for most of his adult life, the first thing Benge wanted to know about was the well.

I think by that time I had already decided to buy the place. So I wasn't really looking for advice, I was looking for support. All I wanted was to hear somebody say that this was the best land deal since God promised Canaan to Moses. There is always a moment in a major undertaking when you get cold feet, and I was at that moment. Before coming west I had read a huge amount of literature about buying country property, and now that I was about to act I couldn't recall a thing. The only questions I could think of were child's questions. Looking around me I saw lots of trees, and so I asked about them.

"What kinds of trees are on the place?" It was a stupid question, but Benge answered in good humor.

"All kinds," he said. "Red fir, white fir, bull pine, tamarack."

You could have said much the same thing about any forty-acre piece of ground between Boise and the Canadian border. North Idaho is timber country; trees are a lot more important to the economy of the state than potatoes. But all I could see at that time were promenades of sharp green tufts stretching around and away in every direction. To my eyes they were all pine trees. I could tell Benge wasn't really interested in the trees. He kept poking around in the grass by the well.

It was mid-May. Northern Idaho was in the soggy green grip of spring, and from the house you could hear the rush of water in the creek. Three days before I'd been mired south of Moscow in mud up to the axles. Muck and rain seemed a permanent fact of life. It was the first time I had ever spent much time in the West, and I was ignorant of the fact that what divides the western half of America from the eastern half is as much water — rather, the lack of water — as anything else.

Later, after having lived for several years in the West, I came to know firsthand on how fragile a base humans exist west of the hundredth meridian. The line does not follow any political borders or obvious topographic features; it more or less bisects the country through the center of the Dakotas, Kansas, Oklahoma, and Texas. It marks a change of climate more than of geography, a shift in the mood of the continent documented nearly two centuries ago by the first European explorers. To the west of that line the air is dry, and, come summer, skies really are not cloudy all day. The brochure I received from the St. Maries Chamber of Commerce mentioned this dryness openly but tersely: "There is a dry rainless period of from three to six weeks in the summer." That was true, although it was not what you would call the whole truth. It would have been more accurate to add that during those three to six weeks in northern Idaho the woods often become tinderboxes, the rivers slow to a trickle, and creeks sometimes vanish altogether.

It took only one year of living in the West to see how closely our fortunes were linked with the weather. In good years — maybe one in seven or eight — our well stayed full or nearly full straight through the summer. But most years it began to empty in early August and did not fully recover until the first snowfall. Our well never ran completely dry, but most summers we had only enough to drink and to cook with. At such times we bathed in the river and left the lawn and the garden in the hands of fortune.

Idaho was always dry in August, and there was nothing wishing or praying could do to change it. At such times you took the long view, wrote off the lawn to the heat and the grasshoppers, and hoped for an early fall and a new winter of heavy snows. Not that we didn't wish for Gulf Coast–style thunderstorms. But the high cirrus clouds of western summers never brought rain. The prosperity of our modern-day homestead in summer depended almost entirely on weather conditions the previous winter. We relied on climate in a way that enforced in our lives a kind of primitive fatalism. What you wanted was a winter that laid down huge amounts of snow and then a long, cool spring that lasted into July to make the snowpack's melting last as long as possible. By the time August had come, the matter had long been decided.

Dick Benge knew all this, of course, but all I saw that day in May was God's greenness. That such lushness was ephemeral was beyond thinking. Benge looked inside the wellhouse, then he poked some more in the brush and grass that sloped down from the springhouse toward the creek. At last he uncovered a spill pipe. Water flowed from it in a steady stream, like a tap turned on halfway. Now we knew we had a well full of water.

"Do you think it's any good?" I asked.

Another stupid question. Why would you dig a well and install a pump just to get bad water? Benge didn't reply. He kneeled down in front of the running water and poked the mouth of the pipe clear of mud and algae. Then he said (and I can hear it even now):

"Well, I reckon here's as good a place to lay as any."

Then he cupped his hands and took a drink.

I know now that Benge was teasing me in the way adults sometimes tease children. My grandfather used to dazzle me by passing his finger through the flame of a candle; years later when I was in high school I learned that if you kept your finger moving, even slowly, you scarcely felt the heat.

It was that way with Benge. He wasn't being particularly daring. You can't live in northern Idaho for fifty years as he had and not recognize the signs of long-term habitation. Around him were the cabin, the fencing, the look of land that has been cared for, abandoned, then cared for again. So he had to know that this little flow of water bubbling out the end of a pipe was the miracle that had made all those other things possible. The wellhouse was tight, the surface of the water inside was clear of debris, and three generations of loggers and farmers must have daily drunk that water. So Benge was just being flamboyant.

But I didn't know that then, and I marveled at his panache. In its context, here in the wilds of Idaho, twenty miles from the nearest town, it wasn't just conversation. It was positively literary. It was an exit line, if an exit line it was to be, worthy of Shakespeare. Shakespeare's characters can be expansive and even flowery, but when they talk about their fates they are eloquent because they are blunt.

Like Feeble, in *King Henry IV:* "A man can die but once. We owe God a death. An't be my destiny, so. An't be not, so."

Or Hamlet: "If't be now, 'tis not to come; if it be not to come, it will be now; if it be not now, yet it will come. The readiness is all."

Benge drank the water. He didn't double over in spasms, not immediately nor on the way back to town nor during the next several days. I didn't drink the water until I'd had it tested. I gathered a sample in a vial I'd obtained from the university health service, drove home with it, and had it analyzed by a laboratory in Pennsylvania. The results were mailed unceremoniously to me two weeks later. The water, in the language of the official report, "conformed to the standards for drinking water." Benge had certainly known that all along. The report noted also that the water contained "incidental bacteria too numerous to count," and I'd bet that Benge, bless his soul, had known that too.

Fences. When Nancy and I moved to Alder Creek in May of 1972 our place had not been farmed seriously for at least a decade, and when a farm is neglected like that the first thing to go is the fences. "Something there is that doesn't love a wall," wrote Robert Frost in one of his two most famous poems, but in many parts of the country it's not walls that are broken by wind and weather but fences. A barbed-wire fence may look trim and mean, but it's surprisingly fragile. If it is to stand, a barbed-wire fence demands vigilance. It is a delicate balance of contradictory materials and forces that needs constant tending. Winter snows weigh down the wires, and spring thaws lift up the posts. Cows strain against it in search of the grass on the opposite side that is always greener. And if the fence runs along the edge of the timber, as fences often do in northern Idaho, a single windfall can take out a hundred yards or more of fence in an instant.

That was the case with the fences on our place. Most of them were fallen or falling. In fact it would be more accurate to say that when we moved to Alder Creek we didn't find fences but rather found places where once fences had stood. Dozens of times we tripped over the remains of an elaborate network of barbed-wire fencing that at one time must have linked yard and pasture and outbuildings in a neat tessellation of split cedar and drawn steel. There were fences to surround a garden or a run for chickens, transecting lines of wood and wire that set off an orchard, a barnyard, and a meadow for horses and goats to graze. It was an image of the wilderness made benign, a rich articulation of the relation between property and nature in western culture. Above all it had character and soul. It is possible to recognize persons by their handwriting or by their gait, and we could read purpose and personality in the traces of a fence.

Not that it was any longer any good. The broken fences served no function but an aesthetic one. They were a constant and pleasingly melancholy image of a pastoral landscape that was making its way back to wildness. The present order, they say, is the disorder of the future. But the fence that enclosed the yard was a different matter. There we needed a fence in working order. At that time Idaho still retained one of the curious legalisms of the early West, the so-called Open Range Law. This piece of legislation had been created in the early days of western expansion. As I understood it, it gave the nineteenth-century cattle barons the right to graze their animals wherever they damn well pleased. We had a couple of such barons *manqué* living around St. Maries, and every summer they would truck hundreds of their cattle to Alder Creek and dump them off to graze. If you were a homesteader and wanted to keep herds of alien cattle out of your meadows and garden, the law said that it was up to you to fence them out.

So one of the things we did was to set about restoring the fence around the yard. At first I tried to match my repairs to the design of the whole, but we were too poor to do that for very long. So I began to make do with whatever materials I had on hand, and soon you could read the fence like a history. It was a sight to inspire amazement and laughter. The fence was mainly barbed wire, like the original, hung on a mixture of wooden and metal posts. But some parts were made of recycled woven wire, and other parts were held together with old telephone lines that I'd salvaged when the General Telephone Company of the Northwest installed its cables underground. About half of the fence contained some waste boards I'd recovered from an old hotel. No two were alike. These were scabbed to each other and to posts or sometimes used to buttress posts that had rotted through at ground level. The entire western side of the fence was made of saplings stretched horizontally and attached to each other and to the uprights by baling wire.

Despite its lunatic complexity, or maybe because of it, it was hard not to admire my fence. People were moved to thoughtfulness by it. It was clearly the work of a desperate amateur, wholly existential, almost like the prayer of a soldier in a foxhole. There was one particularly bad stretch by the well that contained no materials whatever from the first fence. I liked to tell my kids that a fence could be the same fence yet not the same. Like the *Argo*, rebuilt piece by piece even while Jason sailed to Colchis, my fence was a simulacrum. While it was constantly in use, it underwent a complete substitution of components.

You might wonder why I didn't simply build a new fence from scratch. On the face of it, I have to admit it seems strange not to have done just that. It's not necessarily any easier to mend a broken fence than to start over with a new one. And building a brand-new fence has one clear advantage: you can place it to suit yourself. I had no use for a good third of the space enclosed by the old fence, and yet each year for seven years I propped it up one more time. I have no idea why I repeated the old fence except to say that I was moved by the pull of habit. That's where the original fence stood, by God, and that's where I put mine. It follows the same line even now. It's a sobering thought. For almost thirty years I have fitted my life to the fence, not the other way around.

The lesson of the fence is a little like the story I once heard told to describe the civilizing of urban spaces. Say you start with a vacant lot. You start with a little *tabula rasa* of nature, so to speak. But it can't stay that way for long. Sooner or later a dog is going to wander across that lot, and once that dog wanders into unfamiliar territory it's going to want to take a pee. Somewhere, anywhere. But after that random event, things change. All the dogs who wander into that lot forever after will have their own meanderings and peeings set by the activity of the first dog. Grass will flourish in some places, paths will be worn in others, and in time a whole dogdom, like the Roman Empire, will grow, evolve, decline. People arrive, and their decisions and actions of course will be affected by the lay of the land when they got there. And so on. Eventually, goes the story, the entire lot will look the way it does and have the history it does because one day in the dim past some forgotten dog happened to piss in one spot and not any other.

So I once cleared a path through the snow to the barn following the trail my cat had established during her nightly comings and goings. So the Pennsylvania Turnpike, they say, is laid over the game trails of Native American hunters, and so we decorate contemporary courthouses with facsimiles of the garlands the ancient Greeks used to adorn sacrificial oxen. Once things get started they're awfully hard to stop.

Junked cars. In Alder Creek abandoned vehicles were commonly part of the landscape. No homestead lacked them; a few of them were only temporarily immobile, awaiting time and parts; but most had obviously become permanent residents, a peasant's version of garden statuary. In a terrain without street numbers and road signs, these broken machines could also be important navigational tools. Even when these landmarks disappeared, they clung to local memories in the way that long-vanished glaciers are said to influence migrating butterflies. Once, seeking directions to a particular fishing spot, I was told to "go about two miles after where the Caterpillar used to be parked."

We inherited a modest number of junked cars, a Ford and a

Chevrolet. The Ford squatted comfortably in the grass, covered with needles and moss; it seemed profoundly at rest. The Chevy for some unaccountable reason lay on its side. A mystery of people long gone, our own miniature Stonehenge: what hands, what desires had raised that car on its side in the woods? Both cars were the same shade of pale green. Coincidence? Or was this a clue to the personality and taste of our forebears?

Both vehicles were 1953 models, and both were missing their wheels and their hoods. The missing wheels were easy to understand; I didn't know anyone in Alder Creek who had not salvaged wheels and rubber from abandoned cars. But the missing hoods were a puzzle, until years later somebody told me that they had been removed by a tenant during the late sixties. Inverted, their snouts curved sideways and upward in a bow, and in that graceful curving sculpture that desperate tenant saw a sledge that he could use to haul small bits of firewood across snowbound fields.

The cars were nestled more or less together, partly hidden in a grove of white pine and white fir just beyond the south fence line of the yard. You could see them from the kitchen. You would imagine — at least this was what I imagined when I first saw them — that two junked cars would have been an eyesore. But in a short time I came to enjoy looking at them. To see them in no way damaged the visual appeal of the rest of the landscape. On the contrary, the look of them resting there in the grass was oddly comforting. I liked the way they complicated the woods with their presence, and the longer I lived there the more I saw the distinctions between them. They took on character and personality, somewhat like a keepsake. It was a little like having your own family graveyard. To look at them was to remember that you, too, along with all the other golden lads and chimney sweeps and chrome bumpers, must one day come to dust.

Somebody had set a short length of timber across the front fenders of the Ford. It made a fine perch, and all of us went there often. It was a place to retire to think and to smoke, in the days when I still smoked, and after I quit smoking it was still a good place to watch the wind whiffle in the aspens. My daughters played games near it, and later, as they grew up, they sought out the car as a place to sulk or to take friends to smoke and to contemplate adult life.

The cars were a place for mice, for voles, for ants, for ground squirrels, birds, and worms. Pigweed, bristlegrass, and ox-eye daisies grew through the floorboards of the Ford, and in the engine compartment a few white fir seedlings made their way upward around coil springs and steering gear.

And they were places to entertain guests. Once an old friend from the East Coast came for a visit. We had dinner and took a short walk, and then I asked him, What would you like to do for amusement? He thought about it and then replied that if I didn't mind he'd like to go shoot a car.

I was more than a little surprised. You have to understand that this was a person who chose to become a conscientious objector during the Vietnam War. This was a person who once told me it pained him to look at the stuffed head of a deer on the wall. It was a side of him I had not seen, to say the least.

"You want to shoot a car? What car?"

"Yeah," he said. "The ones you got out back. I've always wanted to shoot out a windshield. I think it's all my years living in Brooklyn."

As it turned out, neither of my junkers had a windshield any longer, but there was plenty of glass in the doors and rear. So we took the .22 and a handful of shells out to where the Chevy sat and blasted small holes in the rear window and trunk. By the time we had made six or eight holes each we were both getting into the spirit of the thing, and so I went back inside and got the twelve-gauge shotgun and a box of shells. With that gun we really started to do some damage. We took out the trunk, part of the roof, and, by the time the smoke cleared, most of the back seat. We blasted away for maybe ten minutes, although it seemed to take much longer.

I have to say that it was a deeply satisfying experience.

(3)

Locals

FRIENDS WHO CAME to visit our place in Alder Creek always reported that they had entered another world, one older and more elemental than the one they knew. This impression was not entirely fanciful; there were marked climatological differences between the nearest towns and Alder Creek Flats. Half a thousand feet of altitude separated our place and St. Maries and the university in Moscow. At three thousand feet we experienced spring later and fall earlier than did residents of town; our nights were always colder, and often in the winter what began as rain in town turned to snow as I drove the last few miles home. But these physical distinctions were enhanced by distinct ethical differences. The change was sharp. Visitors from town described a sea change as they traversed Windfall Pass and dropped down into the Benewah Valley. Some reported psychological dislocations, a sense that they had suddenly gone beyond the reach of custom or habit. Others spoke of it in terms of a historical lurch, as if without warning they'd been set down in 1955.

Sometimes when I drove along the Benewah Valley I felt cut loose in time. The valley was full of things that elsewhere had passed into disuse or vanished altogether. It was disarming to drive on a network of dirt and gravel roads, passing other vehicles only occasionally, vehicles in most cases manufactured a decade or two ago yet here still in active service. And when, finally, those cars and trucks ceased to run they were simply put out to pasture like old horses; they were stored out of the way but not out of sight. You had the distinct impression you were on a movie set or in some historical reconstruction; until you got used to it, the feeling could be unnerving. The first time my mother saw the landscape she was transported back to her childhood. "I never thought I'd be on a country lane again," she said in bewilderment.

The first house you passed once you descended into the Benewah Valley belonged to Bill and Cleo McPherson. Squat and unpainted and buttressed all along one side by a pile of firewood nearly as large as the house itself, it looked cheerless and uninviting. But within its walls McPherson sat rocking by his huge double-barreled stove, waiting eagerly for company. McPherson was like the gatekeeper in a fairy tale, full of good humor and gnomic advice. He liked to keep informed about the comings and goings of natives and newcomers alike, and he was pleased whenever people stopped to visit him before continuing about their business. I had never seen a man so dedicated to keeping warm — poor circulation, McPherson explained. He kept his parlor at better than 80 degrees; whenever he couldn't maintain the temperature to his liking, winter or summer, he and Cleo bundled up in their small motor home and headed for a vacation in Death Valley.

McPherson's yard looked like a dump, and it was. I didn't know anyone in Alder Creek who had not sifted through the piles of junk in that yard in search of a tool, a car part, the right piece of scrap metal. The *pièce de résistance* was a towering, faded orange combine. It was a relic from the thirties, something the Joads might have had occasion to operate, and it sat in a corner of McPherson's yard grown thick with weeds and buck brush. Over the years it had come to be an important local artifact. It was part of the plot, like the picture of General Gabler on Hedda's wall or the small chests of family keepsakes in Roman comedy, and McPherson seemed pleased at its notoriety. He once told me about a conversation he'd had at a gas station in California with a stranger. The talk turned briefly to their respective backgrounds, and it turned out that the Californian more than twenty years earlier had worked briefly in the Benewah Valley. His most vivid memory of that part of his life, he said, was driving to work each morning past a house with a faded orange combine parked in the yard.

Even language conspired to create the sense of being in a time warp. In the first months I lived in Alder Creek I heard idioms and pronunciations I had not heard since I was a child in rural Pennsylvania. Words seemed to come from speakers encased in amber. "Creek" was pronounced to rhyme with "sick"; refrigerators were iceboxes, sofas were davenports, and you entertained guests not in the living room but in the front room or parlor. Years later, a colleague of mine at Emory, Lee Pederson, told me that this kind of linguistic preservation often occurs in rural areas, which even in the modern era seem resistant to linguistic shifts.

As for the psychological disorientations, they were harder to identify but no less real. A few of my visitors were deeply upset by rural life. Never before having experienced silence, or isolation, or, deep at night, a truly darkened sky, they lost all bearings. They reverted to the mental apprehensiveness of childhood; the world seemed full of signs impossible to read and sounds impossible to identify. "I can't stand to look at all the trees," a visitor from New York once said. "They scare the hell out of me."

But even people who were familiar with the rural West experienced something close to paranoia. My good friend Sam Riley had grown up in the 1940s outside what was then the little town of Alamosa, Colorado. Yet he too remarked on the peculiar alien ambience of Alder Creek. For him the valley and its residents were a source of amusement; one incident in particular stood out in his memory. It was just at sundown, he said, when one day he drove the last two miles of dirt road to our cabin, and as he made his way around a blind curve he came upon a man riding a mule. The man was old and wore a white beard, but he was neatly dressed in flannel shirt, western boots, and jodhpurs. He was wearing a broad-brimmed hat, and as Riley slowed to pass him, so as not to raise too much dust, the old man turned and very gracefully, almost elegantly but without any irony, swept his hat down and out in a formal gesture of recognition.

"Jesus, Bill," Riley said when he told me about it, "I thought I was in the Twilight Zone. Who was that?"

I told him it was doubtless Duke Martin. "Martin" was the name he chose for an alias. His real name was James Duplessis (something nobody knew until he decided to marry and was required to own up to an actual identity), and he traveled, he always made it a point to tell us, not on a mule but a hinny. Martin lived the life of a hermit about two miles down the road from our place. When he drove, he drove an old Volkswagen bus, but more often than not when he was on local business he preferred to travel on his hinny. It was not only the gesture of tipping his hat, Riley said, that spooked him. It was the whole package — the beard, the riding outfit more suited to a Kentucky thoroughbred than a hinny, and, to top it off, the neatly booted feet resting on a pair of upturned bicycle handles that swung beneath the mount's belly. Riley couldn't get it out of his mind. "Bicycle handles for stirrups!" he kept saying. "I swear, Bill, you'll think I'm crazy, but when I saw those stirrups I could hear somebody playing Flatt and Scruggs off in the distance."

A person in search of local history could do worse than make the turn west off the Benewah road by McPherson's cabin and follow the Benewah Creek past Tom Hodgson's sawmill and up past the old Hodgson homestead. The place was a museum; it was like a *Wunderkammer* such as wealthy Europeans in the late sixteenth century created for themselves by stuffing one or more of their rooms with a motley assortment of booty just off the boat from the New World. Like those chambers, Hodgson's yard was a place for contemplation and study, "a world of wonders in one closet shut."

As you approach it, what strikes you first is the stupefying clutter. Everywhere you look are machines — cars and trucks of course, but also farm and logging implements, hand tools, sleds, carts, great iron-wheeled wagons and trailers — butt ends of logs, sheets of rusting metal, delaminating plywood, drums, cans, boxes, bottles, and pipes. There is no identifiable focus, no center, neither physical site nor ethical purpose that might subtend this wondrous extravagance, and so great is the confusion that it takes you a moment to locate the house. As your eye casts about in search of a dwelling, a command post, you grow anxious, even alarmed. This is no ordinary human disarray but something wilder. In the midst of this vast assemblage of broken things there is not a single functioning object. The crowning touch is a stand of six freshly cut stumps. They look weirdly discordant, the bright yellow disks left by the saw a mystery of recent activity in the midst of overwhelming neglect. It's a summer morning in August, and I pass by Hodgson's place on my way to collect milk from Esta Fletcher. But today I stop first at his son's house. Esta's son Bill lives just up the road from Hodgson, and I'm curious about the stumps. The explanation is obvious to a native: "Kenny logged the yard last week," Fletcher tells me.

I mention this because it is so striking an illustration of the subtle influence culture has on one's sense of household decor. Rural Idaho is not Shaker Heights, and in 1972 in Alder Creek yards like this were common. But I learned to be careful before writing them off as eyesores. Of course it is possible that Hodgson simply didn't care whether or not he saw the beauty of a yard full of trees from his parlor window. But this doesn't preclude him from having at the same time a more "natural" attitude than my own toward his yard, in particular to the extent of viewing it as a site for economic gain. In most cases the aesthetic values we associate with suburban landscapes are the direct consequences of that land's being denied other, more immediately useful functions. I was so accustomed to the sight of single-family houses dominating a half acre or more of mown grass that familiarity prevented me from recognizing how peculiar a disposition of land the suburban yard really is. Among the pleasures of owning land, according to Thorstein Veblen, is seeing perfectly good land taken out of production. But that is a selfish pleasure, one of which we have little right to be proud. Planting zoysia or fescue in front of your house is partly an aesthetic gesture, but it's mainly a way to declare that particular patch of ground unavailable for economic use. Which is of course a way of declaring exclusive ownership of it. Whose attitude toward property, then, was the more honest? My own or Hodgson's?

Everybody who lived along the Benewah Valley and up Alder

Creek seemed to have a clear place in the scheme of things. To live in that small rural environment, with its intricate structure of interrelationships, was to blur the distinction between self and society; it was odd to feel so much a part of the lives of people who were so physically remote. One semester, when my schedule changed and I no longer had to leave the house at 5:30 A.M., I learned that it was widely believed that I'd been laid off from work. My neighbors were accustomed to seeing my car pass by at a certain time each morning, and their lives were disrupted by my change in schedule. For weeks their sympathetic speculations about me and my family traveled the gossip circuit up and down the Benewah Valley.

For someone who had moved from an apartment building where I didn't even know the names of the people on my floor, to become the object of so much interest flustered me; I felt constantly on display, like a kid in a new school. Alder Creek, ironically, was so unpopulated that it was almost impossible to lose touch with yourself and others. I once sat in a jury pool that was being selected to try the case of a youth who'd been arrested for breaking the display window of Charlie's Saw Shop. When asked if she knew the defendant, one prospective juror inquired, "Is that the upriver side of the family?" Neither the judge nor the attorneys thought this degree of familiarity was detrimental to the cause of justice; the question answered, the juror was impaneled and the trial proceeded. Such intimacy between people who lived five or even fifteen miles apart was something everybody took for granted. The mood also extended to strangers; passing cars along the Benewah or Alder Creek Road, I learned to flick my index finger off the steering wheel to wave hello, whether I knew who was driving by or not.

Gossip flowed freely, weaving people and events into a vast collective memory; people's follies as well as their smarter or grander gestures were commemorated in a dreamy and shifting oral network. One old logger was legendary for purchasing hundreds of cans of food each fall, methodically removing their labels and then dining daily on surprises. Individual stories were sometimes made into communal property; several times I heard locals tell about the fantastic sexual initiation a young boy from the Benewah Valley had suffered in the sixties at the hands of two backwoods girls. Ambushed one day in the woods, the story went, the boy was stripped of his clothes, tied to a tree, and pelted with weeds and flowers. The punch line was the same each time — "Of course, up to that time them girls'd never been with anybody but goats" — but each time I heard it, the story involved a different boy.

Even people who anywhere else would have been considered misfits or outsiders were subsumed into the workings of the community. Lowell Radke owned forty acres on Windfall Pass where he kept a small complement of pigs and chickens, selling eggs and occasionally weaner pigs for pocket money. By the time we met him, his third wife was in the process of packing up and moving out. Radke responded by reducing his entire domestic life to the kitchen. That was where he ate, lived, and slept. He invited us inside for coffee; the temperature in the kitchen was freezing, so he turned on all four burners of the electric range to put a little warmth into the room.

Radke was famous for his alcoholic binges. Drink brought out his need for companionship, and he'd lurch into his faded yellow Datsun and cruise the valley looking for society. Fortunately there was never enough traffic on the Benewah Road to make him a danger to anybody but himself. We tried to tell him not to drink and drive, but to no effect: "Hell, whiskey just makes me more alert," he said in complete seriousness. Bill Fletcher told me about the time he'd helped Radke repair some leaks in his roof. They went up to the attic to locate the spots where water was coming in. When Fletcher shined his flashlight on the underside of the roof sheathing he saw that it was all stained black with soot. "What happened up here, Lowell? You have a fire?" he asked. "Nah," Radke said, "when I laid them blocks for the chimney I quit in the attic. I didn't have enough to go all the way through the roof."

On summer weekends, like most of our neighbors, we were always in the forest gathering firewood. These trips became family outings, part of the ritual of rural life. On the outward part of the excursion I liked to ride in the empty bed of the truck; the morning chill filled one with élan. But on the return trip we all squeezed into the cab, and everything else — saw, gas and oil cans, ax, peavey, maul, wedges, water bottles, diaper bags, and bassinet — we piled on top of the wood.

Once we were sitting in the kitchen when a man I had never seen before appeared at the door. His name was Ted Ells, he said, and as was the habit of locals when they began a conversation he also told us the location of his dwelling. "I live in the log house down by John's Creek," he said, and as soon as he said it I knew he meant the cabin that for months had loomed large in our curiosity.

The cabin sat less than five miles from our own, but because of its isolation it seemed much farther away. Beyond traffic and road signs and telephone poles, you have no sense of covering ground as you drive, so even short distances seem very great. When I first saw Ells's cabin, it did not seem possible that there could be anywhere on earth a house so remote. It was built along a trackless spur off the main road, so deep in the timber that it took you by surprise when you saw it. We had come upon Ells's cabin several times, always by accident, and that added to its mystery. For some reason I was never able to find my way directly to it. The house seemed to appear only on its own terms, like the enchanted cottages you read of in fairy tales.

But Ells had come that day with a purpose. Through some network of local gossip he knew us as the family on Alder Creek who had a young baby. "Were you" — and this asocial mountain man put the question with a delicacy so exquisite it might have fit at the court of Versailles — "were you folks perhaps missing a child?"

My newborn daughter was upstairs sleeping in her crib, but that wasn't the first thing that registered on my mind. At that moment she was nowhere to be seen, and so for an instant I felt the deep primal fear of a parent who's suddenly lost track of a child. Then reason returned, and I answered Ells's question. "No, not really," I said. "We're all here." A change came over his face, and he looked embarrassed. "Then I guess all I need to do is return your crib."

The bassinet must have bounced out of the truck that morning without our knowing it. Ells had found it shortly afterward, and, moved by loyalty to a basic social code, left his hermitage no doubt wondering how on earth he could be the bearer of such mournful tidings. Ells must have been relieved to learn that no child had been lost, and he quickly left without saying anything else.

We never saw him again, but now and then I try to imagine his experience on that morning. To the eyes of a woodsman, to eyes accustomed to spotting evidence of loggers or hunters, the empty cans, bits of pipe and chain, shell casings, stains of spilled fluids, the bassinet must have been a marvelous sight. Dali might have painted it: trees, shafts of sunlight, the disappearing curve of the road, and suddenly, gleaming white, a bassinet! Unreal! What had happened? Neglect? Deliberate abandonment? Where were the parents? Worse, where was the baby? A victim of exposure? Taken by coyotes? And what could you say to the mother and father? Did one inquire after misplaced children in the same way one reported stray cattle?

Above all, thinking about Ells's discovery gave us much amusement to imagine how that July morning we must have confirmed an Idaho local's worst suspicions, that those educated hippies in Alder Creek were so no-count as to lose their damn baby in the woods.

If you leave the two-story log cabin belonging to Jim Yearout on the Alder Creek Loop Road and travel east, you can't go a hundred yards without coming upon a small red structure that looks like an old trainman's shack. The building is so small that census takers and surveyors regularly overlooked it; even the electric lines pass by without a break for a transformer and a drop wire. The building has none of the authority that any dwelling in the country possesses just by virtue of its taking over a part of natural space. There is no yard, no fence, no clutter of tools and equipment. The only thing that catches your eye stands out because of its incongruity. Sitting just outside the door is a bright new red Troy rototiller, the *ne plus ultra* of garden equipment in the mind of just about anybody in 1973 who had ambitions for a garden. Except for the tiller, you might mistake the place for a shack for field equipment or a shed for kids to wait for the school bus out of the wind and snow. In this enclosure lived Pat Cady.

Cady was an old man, well past retirement age but with no retirement income to speak of. What money he had he got by working odd jobs in and around Alder Creek. You had the impression that here was a man who had tried his hand at many things and had failed at all of them. Cady was unkempt and rarely shaved or bathed. He belonged to Alder Creek's population of long-term transients. These were people without history, solitary wanderers who drifted into the valley for reasons not always clear or young couples like Nancy and me who came in search of adventure or romance. Sometimes they stayed for years, eventually establishing themselves as second-class natives.

Cady settled rent-free into the shack lent him by the Yearouts. It was for the most part a charitable arrangement, although in Alder Creek as in most rural areas there was always some real advantage to having even an enfeebled caretaker on your property. Cady was arthritic and losing his eyesight, and he spent much of his time fussing with his tiller or looking for refuge in neighbors' houses from whatever tormented him. He sat for hours in people's kitchens, sipping coffee, a lonely soul putting in whatever time was necessary until he could die. He was not particularly conversational, and in some ways his misery seemed to preclude speech. Mostly it was assumed that he could be ignored while you went about your business. But when he spoke, his tongue was surprisingly sharp and, now and then, lewd. He once tried to persuade a young woman to visit him, promising her "the stiffest finger in Alder Creek."

Cady was an odd person to be living in a region where people were more or less accustomed to doing things for themselves. Yet despite his inabilities and his irascible nature, he contributed to the community in intangible ways. Cady was so dependent upon the charity of others that you might have thought he had been set down in Alder Creek to remind us of the biblical injunction to look to the welfare of others as to our own. Here was a man doomed to eternal misfortune, and it was up to us to ensure that he didn't go under.

On top of everything else, one winter night in January of 1975, the creosote in Cady's stovepipe caught fire. Before help could be summoned, the fire ignited the roof of his cabin, and within an hour the house and all it contained had burned to the ground.

Then Cady conceived of his plan to move to Texas. I never learned why he chose Texas. He never spoke of relatives or of personal history in that part of the country. In a curious way his situation reminded me of my own decision to move to Idaho; I think Texas appealed to him for the same reasons Idaho appealed to me, mainly because he knew nothing about it. Like the frontier of American legend, Texas was a dream that captivated Cady at a time in his life when he was feeling vulnerable and out of options.

Through spring and into early June, Cady talked of little else. He would hold forth in great detail about the advantages of life in Texas, and he would complain bitterly about the living conditions in Alder Creek. There was something sadly touching about his litany of complaints — the roads choked with goddamn snow one season and goddamn dust the other, the bastards at Economy Hardware in St. Maries, or his fucking worthless tiller. You sensed in his obscene tirades the man's loneliness, and it was impossible at these moments not to feel pity for him.

Cady's dreams of Texas were one thing, but getting there was another. He had no discernible gift for planning. In a sense, to have his house burn down was a stroke of luck. Suddenly possessed of nothing, you might say, he was spared the rigors of sorting and packing. Still, he had to figure a way to move himself and perhaps fifty pounds of clothes more than fifteen hundred miles, and he was flat broke. He could not fly; he could not afford even a bus. And if he had owned a car, his poor eyesight may well have barred him from obtaining a license. In an age when the ability to traverse continents has become so common as to be almost invisible, Cady's situation was novel and comic. He mulled over various schemes and suggestions, and one day he announced he intended to make the journey by wheelbarrow.

It doesn't take much of a leap to see in Cady the same kind of extravagant caricatures one finds in Samuel Beckett's fiction. When I look back on the years I spent living in Alder Creek it seems to me that they deepened my understanding of literature more than I realized at the time. It was one of a great many things I learned without knowing it. I had the impression that my neighbors resembled figures of fiction and that the two sets of lives, one real and one imagined, ran parallel, on different planes; echoes joined one to the other, enriching and ennobling them both. Living in Alder Creek, I am convinced, opened my eyes to the essential realism of great writers. This does not mean that the only worthwhile literature is based closely on appearances, just that art itself would be absurd if it did not in some way take in everyday feelings and experience.

Once I learned that, I became a much better student and teacher of literature, and I was able to read and enjoy writers whose work had once baffled or bored me. Beckett was not abstract, cold, or intellectual. Like most authors, he was just trying to record life and consciousness as truly as he could. In the Romantic era in Europe, it is said, one could encounter versions of Goethe's Young Werther strolling village streets. I think it is just as easy nowadays to meet versions of Beckett's people, Krapp or Dan and Maddy Rooney or Malone or the Unnameable, muttering to themselves in traffic jams or wandering the shopping malls of the twenty-first century. In this context, the image of an old man, penniless and half blind, pushing a wheelbarrow along Interstate 40 on the way to Texas looks less and less like incidental folly and more and more like a corrective parable for the venial lusts of the age of transportation.

Some time after he announced his plans, Cady sure enough acquired a wheelbarrow. He brought it with him one morning when he came to help Kenny Mullan build an insulated door for his pantry. It was a chilly June morning and several men had congregated at Mullan's place to watch him install the foot-thick door. I was there, and Ed Strobel too. Cady was agitated and adamant; there was no question in his mind that in a few days he would be outward bound. He was just waiting for the good weather.

It dawned on us that maybe he was serious. So Strobel proposed to Cady that he at least practice a little before beginning the trek. It was a well-intentioned suggestion, typical of Strobel, and he put it meekly in the form of an abstract musing. "Maybe a person ought to get used to a trip like this a little at a time? You know, like them runners jog for ten or fifteen miles before they try a marathon?"

Cady seemed not to hear, and Strobel persisted. "Why don't you try to walk your wheelbarrow to, oh, St. Maries?"

Cady turned on him like a cornered animal. "St. Maries?" he bellowed. "St. Maries!" It was hard to tell whether he was angry or surprised or both. "St. Maries! Son of a bitch! St. Maries! Goddamn it, that's twenty miles!"

That was the last we heard of Cady's dreams of pushing a wheelbarrow to Texas. His transformation was complete, almost chemical. Maybe the mention of an actual distance forced him to confront the enormity of what he planned to do. In any case, it was not sour grapes. You could look at him almost fondly, the way a parent views a colicky infant who gives up fighting the moment he sees that his demands are taken seriously. *I never wanted that anyway, all I wanted was for you to believe in me.* To my knowledge Cady never spoke of Texas again, and for the rest of the time he lived in an abandoned house a few hundred yards down the road from the scorched ruins of his shanty.

(4)

The White Fir

SPRING COMES BELATEDLY to Alder Creek. In most parts of the country the progress of spring northward follows reliably and predictably the advance of the solar calendar. If you choose, you can begin in coastal Georgia on the day of the vernal equinox and hike northward at fifteen miles a day, keeping perfect solar time and enjoying for two continuous months the newly opening blooms of dogwood.

But in the mountain regions of the West, altitude matters more than latitude in determining the advent of the seasons, and within a relatively small region you discover extreme differences in climate. Our place lay more than half a thousand feet higher than the town of St. Maries, and so during March and April and well into May, while townsfolk were shedding coats, cutting grass, and tending tomato plants in their gardens, we shivered, built fires at night, and prayed that nothing we'd planted would be so foolhardy as to show its head above ground. Because of our altitude, daffodils and lilacs bloomed weeks after those in the yards of town. Even the trees seemed reluctant to put forth new growth until the balance tipped toward spring late in May. We felt like the selfish giant in Oscar Wilde's story for children, damned to eternal winter because of some basic flaw of spirit.

Often we strolled in the forest even in June to discover small patches of crusty snow lying in dark pockets of brush or beside half-rotten timber. As a result, spring for us was never a distinct season. It was simply a zone of transition from cold to heat, a non-event; it included all the features of the season, but the smells and colors and temperatures were never collected into a unity. Perhaps too because of the dominance of coniferous trees, the spring growth, when finally it came, came so softly as to be almost imperceptible.

There was one exception, in stands of white fir. These trees staged a spring greening unlike any other I'd ever seen, and each year we waited eagerly to see their loveliness.

What we and everybody else in Alder Creek called the white fir, it turns out, is actually something else. The tree properly identified as the white fir, *Abies concolor,* according to all the handbooks and experts I have consulted, grows most commonly in the southern Cascades and the lower and drier elevations of Wyoming, Colorado, Arizona, and New Mexico. What grew in the panhandle of Idaho was a related but distinct species. Handbooks and logging scale slips identify this tree as the grand fir, *Abies grandis.* Full grown, *Abies grandis* is a magnificent tree; at maturity it can tower 150 feet above the duff of the forest floor, with a girth more than twelve feet.

But it's not its size that makes the white fir stand out in the forest. Other trees grow taller or take on more substantial girths — the white pine and the ponderosa pine regularly achieve bigger proportions. And as far as trees go, the white fir's lifespan is unremarkable. White firs live, on average, only a couple of hundred years. However much humans might envy that span of years, amid the company the white fir keeps an organism that dies after a mere two centuries must seem as evanescent as a butterfly. The western larch (which we called the tamarack) easily lives into its fifth century, and the western red cedar can often endure upright for more than a millennium.

But I know no other tree that is so perfect to view. If you drive the back roads of Benewah County and run your eyes along a ridge of trees, their shapes illuminated against the deepening gray of a winter's dusk, it is the white fir you would be most likely to notice. Its chief feature is its beautiful spire-like form, which it retains well into maturity, and its branches sweep down and outward in bows so gently curved as to seem almost weightless. In the silhouette of the white fir you would see, almost as if abstracted, symmetry, order, grace.

It is that perfect, the white fir. Even its needles are striking: they are a deep green, broad and flat and somewhat darker than the needles of most of the other trees in northern Idaho, and their undersides are a shiny, almost silvery white. The tree has an intense fragrance, especially the bark; I have read that old-time woodsmen often had faith in the healing powers of the pungent liquid they pinched from resin blisters on the bark of young white fir trees. Of course they were pinching the bark not of *Abies concolor* but of *Abies grandis.*

The misnomer comes about because language bends under the strains of individual usage. There is an element of laziness in this. The men who felled trees for a living in northern Idaho in the early twentieth century were not overly concerned with the subtleties of scientific nomenclature. What looked to them like the white fir they had been cutting last year on the Clearwater River simply became the white fir of the Idaho panhandle; let the specialists figure out the difference.

Residents of Alder Creek referred to two kinds of trees as fir trees — the white fir, which of course was a misnomer, and the "Doug," or Douglas fir, which it turns out is not a fir at all but only looks like one. It is a pseudo-fir, apparently, from its scientific name, *Pseudotsuga menziesii.* What preacher could devise a lesson in worldly folly more comic, more humbling? Humans call a true fir by its wrong name and unfairly promote an impostor to genuine fir status. And there is one final irony: the white fir — grand fir, of course — is not highly valued for its wood, which is considered too soft to make much of anything but paper. As if to compensate for its relative valuelessness, it grows swiftly and in denser stands than other trees, and so it prevailed in much of the forest. On our place, more than half the stands of timber were dominated by the white fir.

Nevertheless, in some ways the white fir was the tree that gave us the most pleasure. In spring, at the tips of each branch a dense tuft of pastel green needles appears. So strong is the contrast between these tips and the deep background shade of the older foliage that the whole tree gives the appearance of having been lightly frosted, or of having suddenly brought forth countless artists' brushes dipped in bright green paint.

The effect is emphatically artificial, and we enjoyed it immensely for that reason. It's proof of the paradox that nature most delights human eyes when it somehow appears unnatural. When we admire a landscape, we often as not are pleased to see nature look like artifice. We call it scenic, from *skene* — the tent, later a wooden façade, behind the stage on which Greek tragic actors played in the fifth century B.C.E. For similar reasons, Nancy and I enjoyed walking or driving among stands of tamaracks in Alder Creek in late fall. The tamarack is rare among conifers in that it behaves like its distant deciduous relatives, shedding bright yellow needles each autumn, and in the midst of a grove of tamarack the fallen needles blanket the ground so completely as to carpet it in bright gold. At such times we were not moving through the real world; we were in legend and myth. We walked in the wood outside Athens in *A Midsummer Night's Dream,* we strolled through Tolkien's Rivendell, we belonged to the court at Camelot.

The pleasure we found in these moments makes me feel a little more tolerant of those crazy Victorians whose idea of enjoying the natural world was to look at it with a Claude glass. This viewing device was named after the seventeenth-century painter Claude Lorraine, whose canvases of hazy skies and misted plains so appealed to nineteenth-century tourists that they carried with them on their travels a smoked convex mirror in which they viewed — thus suitably romantically transformed — the natural scene on which they'd turned their backs. It sounds silly, but maybe they were on to something. In much the same spirit, my son tells me he likes to look in the wing mirror of the car when we take trips; he often prefers, he says, to look at the passing landscape as it is framed and distanced by the convex glass.

We would drive along logging roads late in May just to see the spectacle of the white fir in bloom. Within a stand of such trees, if the light was just right, low and late in the day, the forest became picturesque and ethereal. You could easily believe that the whole landscape burned with a green fire, yet without smoke or heat, and all in perfect silence. The color would persist for as much as a week, and then, as Robert Frost, in "Nothing Gold Can Stay," said of leaves, dawn, and Eden, the loveliness of first things subsided, and we knew it was summer.

5

Immigrants and Emigrants

WHEN, in March of 1972, I told friends in Philadelphia that I was moving to northern Idaho, one of them asked me, "What's the neighborhood like?"

It was the only time in my life when I understood how King Louis must have felt when he famously claimed that he and all of France were identical. "I *am* the neighborhood" was my answer. And it was true.

The region around Alder Creek had gone through two successive waves of European settlement. First came the idealistic homesteaders of the early twentieth century, and later came the desperate migrants of the Depression. But by midcentury few of these early settlers remained, and over the ensuing decades their properties had been bought up and consolidated by timber corporations or by one man, Andrew Brede. Brede had patiently built up his holdings in Alder Creek until he controlled better than three thousand acres. Our own place was an island in the sea of his ranch. But Brede farmed mainly in Washington, where he controlled an even greater estate, and so in his view the Alder Creek ranch was little more than a vast private summer range for cattle.

The Brede ranch house, the last outpost to be served by the telephone and electric lines, sat empty for much of the year. Beyond it the county road ran eastward for another five miles through country known locally as the Alder Creek Flats. The land all along the road and for at least a half mile deep on either side was in the hands of Brede. Eventually Brede's pastures gave way to timbered land owned by the Milwaukee Railroad; the change in ownership was marked, probably not coincidentally, by a change in the composition of the road from gravel to dirt. It degraded into a ruinous track known to us as the River Road. From there, for another five miles it descended slowly by a series of dizzying switchbacks till it bottomed along the St. Maries River and headed toward town.

Almost none of that country was inhabited then; our nearest neighbors lived about two miles distant on the Alder Creek Loop Road. This was an ancillary spur off the main county road that for some reason had collected all the people, somewhat like the business loop of an interstate highway. The only residents for miles around who lived on the main road were the hermit, Duke Martin, and the Gronseths, a mother and her two middle-aged daughters, who lived a pioneer-style existence at the extreme eastern edge of Brede's holdings. Their cabin lay six miles beyond the Brede ranch house; once in a great while, it was said, they walked to town, returning with several months' worth of supplies on their backs, including, once, a cast-iron stove.

All that changed in the summer of 1973, when Andrew Brede sold his Alder Creek ranch to a land development company that called itself Reforestation, Inc. The name was a marketing sham, naturally; I doubt that the company ever planted a single tree. It intended to appeal to a generation of people who believed that the country was undergoing a "green revolution," and it placed ads in local newspapers as well as in national publications such as *Four Wheeler* and *Field & Stream*. And soon, lured by the same kinds of visions of material wealth and spiritual fulfillment that have inspired several centuries of American westering, the immigrants began to arrive in Alder Creek. Some of them were just curious to view their estates firsthand. They drove to their forty acres, walked about, and left to let their investment mature. Others came for a vacation; they cut driveways through the brush, threw together a campsite, and erected a makeshift mailbox and a clothesline. And a few were genuine immigrants. They came with ambitions of permanent residency, and they had every intention of moving "back to the land." They were bent on living an American idyll, carving a working homestead out of the wilderness.

All of the immigrants to Alder Creek tried to build houses of one sort or another. We visited all those construction sites at least once, either while they were being built or after their makers had departed. The backgrounds of the builders could not have been more varied. Some came from the East, bringing impressive amounts of money and education. Others, sometimes from California but more often from rural Washington or southern Idaho, brought little more than their youth and their dreams. Among the things I have kept from the years I stockpiled material about life in Alder Creek is a set of my photographs of those constructions. Some picture elaborate log or frame skeletons, others show crude lean-tos or low-roofed shanties, still others reveal only the remnants of a foundation. The black-and-white photographs narrate themselves; mostly it is their awkwardness and their ordinariness (the result of my own lack of artistry) that make them documentary. Also their emptiness: because the pictures lack human subjects and subjectivity, they somehow become all the more representative of their makers and register flatly the elegant strangeness of daily life in Alder Creek.

One snapshot shows the eight-foot-high walls of what was to be the foundation of the house of Alan and Liane Belko. The block walls enclose a full basement with a poured concrete floor, perhaps twenty by forty feet. Compared to other Alder Creek foundations, which if they existed at all were simple posts or rows of unmortared concrete blocks, this foundation was a work of great labor and expense. It was the local version of the ruins of Ozymandias. In my photograph the concrete floor is scarcely visible, for it is covered by trash, mostly tin cans, in places a foot deep. When at last it became clear to Alan and Liane that the home they planned would never be finished, they used the empty basement as a place to throw their refuse.

Alan and Liane Belko came to Alder Creek from Germany in the spring of 1974. Belko was American, the son of a career soldier; Liane was the daughter of a minor German consular official. She had followed her new husband to the rural American West, to a place that must have seemed, in the eyes of someone accustomed to the orchestrated spaces of continental Europe, the wastelands at the end of the earth. With what hopes or anxieties Liane participated in her husband's experiment in primitivism, I never knew; she rarely left their trailer house, except for the occasions when she came to our place to borrow the telephone. They lived first in a huge army-surplus wall tent they erected on their land and later in a mobile home they had trucked to their building site, about a quarter mile south of the back end of our place. Liane seemed to put all her energy into crafts, so that within a few months the front room of their trailer overflowed with small crocheted dolls and glossy ceramic curios. The inside of the trailer was Liane's world, and when you entered it you could not help but think that you were entering a space created solely to offset the loneliness and emptiness that lay just outside the door. Outside the trailer, the forest and the mountain ridges stretched east in uninterrupted rows for nearly half a thousand miles. Inside the trailer were a multitude of ceramic dwarves and animals, woven wall hangings and antimacassars, books, German magazines, even a cuckoo clock.

Unlike most other immigrants, the Belkos brought with them enough money to secure their future. They bought four contiguous forty-acre plots to make up a full 160 acres, the traditional size of western homestead grants; their land lay a quarter mile off the county road. They bought a new Volkswagen bus, a new Ford three-quarter-ton pickup truck, a mobile home, and a mountain of power tools, farming implements, and construction equipment. Everything was paid for, or so the story went, with cash they'd brought with them. The money was rumored to be more than $100,000, the sum paid to Belko by an insurance company as settlement for injuries he had received in a motorcycle accident in Germany. That much money was beyond comprehension for a graduate student who lived on veterans' education benefits and an annual stipend from the university of $2,800. It was beyond comprehension even if I allowed myself the luxury of dreaming that I might be one of the lucky four out of ten graduate students who actually got a full-time teaching job when they finished their Ph.D.

Belko made no attempt to find work. He planned to spend his capital until he and his wife had turned their 160 acres of timber and meadow into a self-sustaining farm.

Rumor had it that Belko had once been brilliant and genial but that the accident had changed him in ways that were difficult to fathom. He was handsome and scruffy at the same time, a little like Jim Morrison of The Doors. He carried, so he said, a stainless-steel plate in his skull. The injuries he'd suffered in the accident had left him with a distinctive slowness of response, and in dealing with him you had the impression he was rediscovering even simple acts. He talked softly and without any real pace or rhythm, and he sometimes paused in midsentence or even midsyllable, as if he were looking for the way to complete a word or continue a line of thought. And there were times when his personality appeared to be an artificial construction, the way it is with adolescents or two-year-olds who sometimes try on different voices and roles.

Belko had much bitterness in him that he seemed to be trying to work through, and his difficulties in speaking seemed only to inflame his half-buried anger. He never raised his voice or acted with violence, yet I had never seen a man more habitually belligerent. It was impossible to hold a conversation with him. No matter what the subject, Belko held an opinion that he was prepared to defend against wisdom, reason, or published documentation. He knew about welding, animal husbandry, and modular housing. More than once he denounced multigrade motor oil, slightly higher-priced than single-grade oils, as a greedy trick of the petrochemical industry.

"Twenty-W-forty oil," Belko insisted, "is half twenty-weight and half forty-weight oil." He made it sound logical, so purely inspired, as if he'd had a revelation, like Newton's insight into gravity. "I make it myself," he confided. "All you do is mix together three quarts of twenty-weight oil with three quarts of forty-weight. Those bastards aren't going to get my money."

Yet you couldn't help but feel affection toward Belko. We didn't pity him because of his misfortune; we came to prize his comic belligerence. His presence added something tangible to Alder Creek; if the world was indeed a stage, Belko's part was necessary. Enid Welsford has written of clowns and court jesters that "their folly is regarded not merely as a defect but as the quality which endears them to the community," and in the fifteen months that Belko lived in Alder Creek he was in many ways a local reincarnation of the legendary European figure of Unreason.

Belko was the only person I knew who had actually felled a tree on top of his truck. By some combination of ignorance and inattention and sheer bad luck, one afternoon, gathering firewood, he had brought two tons of red fir smashing down onto the bed of his brand-new four-wheel-drive pickup. The back half of the truck was crushed beyond hope of repair. For most people, the accident would have meant a crippling financial loss. Even worse, their shame would have been bottomless. Felling a tree on your truck was considered the most absurd of all woods blunders. It was north Idaho vaudeville.

Belko had to know this. But he never seemed embarrassed by his folly. When we teased him about it he patiently and formally explained how it had happened. There was nothing hangdog or shamefaced about him, and the artificial way he recited the story gave him a weird authority: "Before I know it — boom!" All the while he was talking, he looked at us with a twinkle in his eyes, as if to inform us that this was no simple blunder but some crazy triumph. You could almost believe he had meant to do it. It was an instance of what philosophers call the higher slapstick: sublimely comic, lyrical, rejuvenative.

In a few days Belko, in his usual deliberative manner, removed the crushed bed from the back of his truck and scrapped it. Then he bolted a platform of four-inch-thick planks to the back of the chassis. The whole thing was disproportionate: it looked like Huck's raft had somehow mated with a Ford 350, or like a child's drawing of a person, all head and everything else vestigial. The truck became wonderfully strange, a clash of incongruous arts. At the front was the avant-garde of automotive design, a contoured sculpture in steel, plastic, and shimmering clear-coat green; to the rear were entirely different styles and textures, rough-sawn cedar and hard right angles, all fitted together with lap joints and carriage bolts according to a technology of construction that hadn't changed much since the age of water power.

There was nothing particularly odd about Belko's strategy. His makeshift truck was like my makeshift fence; in Alder Creek, bricolage was a common solution to misfortune. What was uncanny about this near disaster is the way the characters of the modified truck and Alan Belko seemed to blend. Each wounded near annihilation, then rebuilt, man and truck independently seemed to have arrived at some corresponding bedrock of themselves. They were mirrors, kindred spirits. If there exists some higher principle that reconciles motor vehicles and their owners, this was surely the truck Belko was destined to have. For months afterward with precise and unflappable aplomb Belko drove his truck in and about town and the valley. You might have thought that such had been his intention all along.

Another time I was with Belko when he tried his hand at dynamite. He wanted to make way for a yard around his house, and there were dozens of very large stumps, left there when the land was first logged early in the century, in his way. None of his neighbors owned a Caterpillar big enough to budge them, so Belko concluded he would have to blast the stumps out.

I had no experience with explosives, and I was appalled when Belko announced that he'd bought some dynamite for his stumps. Still, like everyone else up and down the valley, I found time during the next week to go watch Belko blow holes in his future front yard.

The whole enterprise had the heady promise of a saturnalia. How was a man who had felled a tree on his truck going to manage dynamite? We watched, drank coffee or beer, chatted with Liane or each other, paused to listen to the *whooof!* when Belko shouted "Fire!" and set off another charge. This atmosphere of public spectacle had its darker side, of course. Most of us fully expected that Belko would somehow bungle the task — let me say right away, he did not — and we assembled around the edge of his property, waiting, like the chorus in a Greek tragedy, for the catastrophe we all felt was soon to come.

On the day I visited Belko's operation I positioned myself about a hundred yards from the location of the blasting, far enough to see the explosion before I heard it. When the sound reached me it was surprisingly muffled and dull, completely out of proportion to the power I had seen. The whole thing seemed out of harmony. For the few seconds between the blast and the smashing return to earth of the broken stump, everything seemed to be taking place in slow motion. The temporal retardation happened with each blast, and for me this was the most fascinating part of the whole thing. I saw events objectively, moving within a purely aesthetic realm, as sometimes occurs when you watch dancers who keep time to a melody you cannot hear.

That fall, Belko became convinced that happiness lay farther west; he left Alder Creek still pursuing the myth of the Garden of the West one hundred years after the frontier was officially closed. He and Liane bought a small farm on Vashon Island in Puget Sound. So far away, so self-consciously rural (accessible only by ferry, Vashon Island lay scarcely five miles to the west of the Sea-Tac airport), the location seemed the ideal location for a postmodern homestead. There were blackberries in abundance, Belko said, fertile soil, short winters, and limitless water.

The last time I saw them they were setting out for town in their Volkswagen bus. Snow was falling, big, dense flakes; it had fallen through the night, and by midmorning it lay six inches deep on the car. They offered to drive me out to the road. It was a pleasure to sit on a clean, soft seat and smell the vinyl and unsullied upholstery — I hadn't been inside a new car in years. The last thing I remember is watching Belko clear the snow from the windshield with his wipers. I had never seen wipers so powerful. It was a miniature epiphany: one minute thick snow obscured the glass, the car's interior was hushed and dim; then suddenly light flooded the passenger compartment, the outside world swung into view, and for a moment you could believe in the future and the limitless promise of money and technology.

Another couple who moved near us in Alder Creek were Annie and Mike Lloyd. Annie was the daughter of one of the then assistant secretaries of state, and Mike's father, though Mike spoke of him reluctantly so that you sensed there was some bad feeling between them, was a successful Hollywood producer. The Lloyds too bought land, and they too had available to them large sums of money. But unlike Belko, the Lloyds viewed their wealth skeptically, and as a result I think they were happier in the few years they lived in Alder Creek.

I think they brought with them around $30,000. But during the entire two years they lived in northern Idaho they ignored their bank account and lived close to poverty. And while they lived on next to nothing, they worked like demons. They built a cabin about ten feet square and lived in it without electricity or plumbing. Most rural shacks look like shacks, blights on the landscape, but the Lloyds' cabin was appealing to the eye. Looking at it, you often felt a silly grin spreading over your face, it was so perfectly miniaturized, so damned cute. It was a child's playhouse, a doll's house.

Mike Lloyd was determined to be a writer, but he had no time to write. The days he was not laboring mightily to turn rangeland into fertile soil he drove a semitrailer, earning what little cash they would allow themselves to spend by hauling truckloads of wood chips from the mills in Coeur d'Alene to the chipboard plants in Lewiston. Five days a week he drove back and forth over two-lane blacktop roads that were often, as he put it, "slicker than snot." Weekends and evenings he and Annie took turns running their John Deere Model A tractor, the famous "Poppin' Johnny" of the thirties and forties. Again and again they ran the tractor back and forth over their fields, disking and redisking the tough sod so as to make it fit for planting barley. With the barley harvest from eighty acres, they hoped to bank enough profit to live from one year to the next. Many summer nights as we went to bed we could hear the distinctive *pop-pop-pop-pop* of the Lloyds' tractor working the fields, their only illumination the moon and a single six-volt running light.

People who knew of the Lloyds' money could not comprehend their unwillingness to spend it. They saw their enforced poverty as foolishness, and a few even denounced them privately for hoarding. There were times when I resented the Lloyds because what was for them a game was my reality. Like most of the people in Alder Creek, I didn't have to pretend I had no money. It is easy to endure poverty when you know it's only temporary. But in retrospect the Lloyds' behavior seems to me less an instance of fashionable slumming than a rigorous exercise of mind and soul.

I always connect the Lloyds with a rare kind of literary form, a work called a lipogram. A lipogram can be a poem or story, short or long, history or fiction. All you have to do to write one is to avoid using one letter of the alphabet. It's your choice as to which letter, though naturally somebody who writes a sonnet omitting the letter *z*, say, is not going to be challenged as much as someone who decides to compose a four-hundred-page novel without one of the vowels.

The form dates as far back as the sixth century B.C.E, the invention, according to tradition, of a lyric poet named Lasus (born in Athens in 548 B.C.E.), but the list of writers who have mastered it is, not surprisingly, not lengthy. Tryphiodorus, a Greek writer of the third or fourth century C.E., is said to have composed a lipogrammatic *Odyssey*. More recently, Georges Perec in 1969 published a novel, *La Dispirition*, denying himself the use of the letter *e*. (The work has now been translated into English and heroically preserves Perec's original omissions. Its title: *A Void*.)

Among readers, the common reaction to such masochistic extremes of literary endeavor is scorn. Addison, in the eighteenth century, once wrote an essay in the *Spectator* in which he denounced the ancient letter-droppers for their false wit. But I think Addison missed an important point of literary creation and maybe also of ethics. Perec did not believe that in abandoning *e* he was denying himself the opportunity for meaningful expression.

On the contrary, he says, the loss was actually a gain. It was, he says, "not a handicap, not a constriction, but, all in all, a spur to my imagination." And Perec's translator seems to have discovered the same paradox. He too tells how, by way of his apparent sacrifice, he discovered an unexpected freedom. "It forced you down certain paths," he says, "which you would otherwise never have taken."

It was the same way with Mike and Annie Lloyd. Forsaking their bank account was an act like the lipogrammaticist's renunciation of a critical letter or a medieval ascetic's denial of the world. The choice is binding and unequivocal. You either do without and find your goal or your god, as the case may be, or you indulge yourself in the abundance of earthly things and maybe are lost. I don't want to sound pompous or mystical about this — it's too easy to think that character and wisdom matter more over the course of life than sheer good fortune. But it seems worth recalling here the ancient notion that material wealth and spiritual poverty go hand in hand. Of all the immigrants who came to Alder Creek and subsequently left, Mike and Annie Lloyd alone departed without leaving behind them evidence of effort spent in vain dreams.

In the fall of their first year in Alder Creek, the Lloyds harvested a crop of barley, and they banked a profit from their crop sufficient to take them through the winter. The next year they did it again. And then, having proved to the world, but more importantly to themselves, that living on the land by dint of one's labor was no dream, they sold their farm to Andrew Brede's old ranch foreman and returned to California.

What did they leave behind? On the surface, not much. Twenty years later, the land bears no sign of ever having been inhabited. The home site is empty, gone back to brush and an aspiring stand of bull pine. The field has returned to timothy and hawkweed, and the place lacks the sorry assortment of trash that always seems to accumulate on rural homesteads. There are no metal drums and empty oil cans and broken tools, no scraps of plastic and aluminum, no detritus of modern packaging, not a single abandoned vehicle. Looking at what was once their place, you would find it hard to imagine that anyone ever lived there, and in a way that is the best thing anyone can ever do for the land.

Still, if you know where to look and what to look for, you can find traces. Now, as you drive along the Benewah Valley and up the Alder Creek Road, you will see here and there a field that for decades was considered fit only for occasional pasture planted in grain. In most years the farmers harvest a crop. We sometimes forget that the most important thing we can do with our lives is to make them models for somebody else to follow. Before the Lloyds proved that it was possible to grow grain in Alder Creek, no one imagined that it could be done. Knowing this small part of the history of Alder Creek, you derive some satisfaction in seeing a handful of flinty souls turned from doubt to faith. No one is as yet planting okra and tomatoes, but lesser things can be done.

And then there is their cabin itself. That now stands in a different place. Dan Hay, who bought the Lloyds' property when they moved, trucked the tiny structure three miles down the road, just south of the corral at his ranch. He keeps it there, unused but still, after a quarter century, in good repair. It sits beyond the fence in its own public space, its storybook diminutiveness a kind of local monument.

6

Falling Trees

I ASKED Dick Benge once what he thought about the practice of selective logging. "Hell, yes," he said. "We did it all the time. You select a mountain and you log it."

The speech of the loggers I know has much the same characteristic brevity, wit, and understatement. Loggers are inherently suspicious of neologisms, which they invariably interpret as just one more instance of bureaucratic meddling in their affairs. They mistrust abstractions; their speech is anchored in the material world. Asking questions of loggers, you invariably receive a sequence of odd material details in reply. The first time I went to cut firewood I asked Kenny Mullan how much wood we were likely to find. It was admittedly a stupid greenhorn question, like asking after the number of fish in the sea. Mullan replied simply that I'd find "enough wood to pop the wheels off your truck."

It was a description I took then as local hyperbole, but almost thirty years later I learned to my chagrin that once upon a time I had been told the literal truth. It was indeed possible to put enough weight on the back of a truck to break the bead that seals the tire to the rim. One late afternoon in August of 1999 I crammed my truck so full of firewood that the great weight squeezed the left rear tire loose from the wheel, releasing all the air. As I labored in the heat to offload the wood so as to be able to raise the rear end with my jack, I remembered with humility how much I'd learned in Alder Creek about the way the world works.

Harvesting timber is such an ancient and ongoing activity that one would expect to encounter no problems talking about it, so it is a little surprising to discover that contemporary English is strangely vague when it comes to naming those people who cut down trees. As a descriptive term, "loggers" is inaccurate. "Loggers" refers to people who make their living harvesting timber, and the term includes, in addition to the few workers who actually fell the trees, a small army of operators of various types of machinery. "Sawyers" sounds too formal for backwoods use, and "woodchoppers" and "woodcutters" belong only in fairy tales. And "fellers," though it may be etymologically correct, is not in any dictionary. That leaves "fallers," which is what most of the men call themselves if they are asked. As for what they do, they fall — not fell — trees. They admit no difference between "falling" and "felling," which is to say that their terminology reaches back more than a thousand years, to the time before Anglo-Saxons split off *feallan* (to cause to fall) from *faellen,* to fall down.

When loggers speak about themselves and their trade they speak in fragments and conditionals and weirdly distorted arrangements of verb tense. To the overly educated, such speech is taken as a sign of general ignorance. But often the speaker's awkwardness with words belies a subtle and thoughtful mind, and more than once a piece of mangled syntax struck me as a novel attempt to grapple with existential complexities. Once, in response to my question about the status of a road, I was told that "a fellow used to could've came through there," and I understood the speaker instantly and perfectly. It was just one more case where proper grammar might have misrepresented what was meant. Illiteracy, so exaggerated, can become eloquence.

I have yet to meet a logger who felt comfortable speaking more than three sentences in a row, or whose sentences are not made up mostly of pauses. And when, rarely, a logger expresses an opinion, it's usually phrased as a conditional. The first time he stopped by our place, Jim Yearout sized up our truck: "A fellow'd want to cinch up them lug nuts real tight," he said. The hesitancy with which he told us we were risking our lives with unsafe equipment was typical of a logger's demeanor. More often than not, the loggers from whom we sought woods advice were reluctant to express an opinion at all. It got to the point where we made fun of their standing answer to inquiries about the state of affairs on any subject between heaven and earth: "A fellow wouldn't want to say."

Such taciturnity, like their haphazard grammar, is not a sign of dullness; it's more like a symptom of an essential deliberateness of spirit. My guess is that if they're not born with a predisposition to caution, loggers come by it through their trade. Logging is in many ways like testing an unfamiliar aircraft; both jobs are statistically among those occupations most likely to kill their practitioners, and both, therefore, demand full concentration. In the woods, as in the air, things happen without warning, and if they happen when your attention has flagged momentarily, the likely result is blood and gore. I have seen grizzled sawyers of more than thirty years' experience use their chain saws with the caution of a *Consumer Reports*–reading suburbanite.

Yet a logger is somebody who loves his work even though he knows that it may well kill him. It's not like being a mechanic or carpenter. In those occupations, the better you are, the easier things get and the quicker you become at doing them. In theory, the best sawyers are the quickest, but in the woods the quicker you saw down trees, the more likely the possibility of a dangerous miscalculation. It's no great trick to cut down a tree, even a big one, if it's standing by itself and you have a whole morning to do it. Beavers do this all the time; they hack away at the thing till it falls down — falls down somewhere, anywhere. But the task is infinitely harder when you're working your way up a steep and heavily forested slope, trying to thread each falling tree through the six or eight others nearby that must remain standing and unscarred, paying attention all the while to the half-dozen other sawyers, chokesetters, and skidder operators in your vicinity. To do all this efficiently takes a great deal of concentration and forethought, and it's when you're tempted to think about where to drop the next three trees you're planning to fell even as you're finishing the cut on the first one that you risk the moment of inattention that someday just might kill you.

Not much of this ever makes its way into the public consciousness. The myth surrounding the logger nowadays depends on outdated notions of maleness as well as the widespread assumption that anyone who cuts down trees has a callow disregard for the land. Three decades of ecological awareness have perverted the image of the logger into a greedy and uncaring despoiler of the landscape. But like most of the images circulated and popularized by the media, the myth of the logger as destroyer is seriously flawed. The loggers I knew locally had no intention of turning the countryside into grassland.

Many of the men I met were first-generation immigrants or the sons of immigrants to the Northwest. Loggers came to the panhandle of Idaho some decades after the miners had come in search of quick fortunes in gold and silver, and the difference in their motives for emigrating was reflected naturally enough in fundamental differences in behavior. The majority came from the upper Midwest or the northern plains states — Wisconsin, Minnesota, Kansas, and the Dakotas — and so they brought with them the Scandinavian or northern European patterns of living and architecture common to that part of the country. They built log cabins — not log houses — with round logs and square corners, they bore names such as Marquardt, Hodgson, and Yearout, and they were predominantly farmers rather than ranchers. They not only cut down trees on their land, they and their families lived on that land and in it, and over the course of a lifetime they came to know more and care more about the health of the land than many of the enlightened urbanites who now dot the landscape with retirement houses and expensive vacation homes. Once the Benewah County road crew dozed out a couple of miles of wild roses that grew in profusion along a stretch of the Benewah Road. The object was to prevent snowdrifts from piling up against the hedgerows, but locals saw only needless despoliation. Tom Hodgson, the owner of a local sawmill and a logger for more than half a century, said simply and sadly, "They took our roses." He sounded bewildered, near tears.

Since the fifties, the tool of the trade for a logger has been the chain saw. Unlike most other tools powered by small gas engines — lawn mowers, brush trimmers, and leaf blowers — the chain saw remains largely undomesticated. Using a chain saw makes you redefine your ideas about the cultural implications of the internal combustion engine. On the one hand, the chain saw is a marvel of technology. The day I bought one, I brought it home and set it on the floor of the cabin and stared at it for more than an hour in disbelief. I swear the saw had an aura around it, an edge between it and me, as if I and it were not in quite the same space. I couldn't find any way to connect the diminutive innocence of the thing's looks with the knowledge that this metallic assemblage was to be responsible for keeping me and my family warm. Small, powerful, and light — it weighed no more than a large house cat — it could cut a winter's worth of wood with less than a gallon of gas and a half-hour spent sharpening the chain.

But that magical power comes at a price. Anybody who uses a chain saw makes a tacit bet against his own good fortune. Chain saws are simple enough that any person can use them, but unlike any of the other power tools commonly in use in modern America, a chain saw cannot ever be made safe for its user. The cutters spin around a steel bar, fully exposed, inches from your hands, head, and feet, and the moment you let down your guard those terrible whirling teeth will likely as not find a twig or splinter to bind on, and quicker than you can possibly react, the saw will be headed full throttle toward your face, or if you are especially unlucky, the femoral artery in your thigh. A chain saw is forever looking for ways to get you.

These feelings weren't entirely a greenhorn's phobias; most of my neighbors felt the same way about their saws. "It should be illegal for fools to buy them," says Peter Leschak, in *Letters from Side Lake*, "and anyone who buys one is a fool." The first time I used a chain saw I was under the tutelage of Kenny Mullan. Early in the summer of 1972 Mullan contrived to accompany me each time I set off to cut wood.

Mullan was proud of his knowledge of the ways of the woods. He'd started work the year before as a "greaser" for the Potlatch Lumber Corporation, which is a sort of entry-level job offered when times are good to just about anybody who walks in off the street. Soon he was promoted to mechanic, and eventually to shop foreman. He was technically unschooled, but his mind was sharp,

and over the course of several careers, ranging from navy elec-
tronics to air conditioner repairman, he had absorbed huge
amounts of information. Mullan was adept at fixing whatever
broken things came his way; it didn't matter whether it was a hair
dryer or a Cummins diesel engine. Machinery was the passion
that ran through the various aspects of his life. Mullan had an al-
most childlike love for taking things apart, and when he talked
about machines he spoke from the heart. "There's two things I
never lend out," he said one day, without context and in what
couldn't have been more than our second or third conversation.
"My chain saw and my wife."

Most of the people I knew in Alder Creek talked about their
chain saws as if they had both personality and will. During the
years we lived in Idaho I owned three different saws and regularly
used four or five others, and they all seemed to have minds of
their own. They looked docile; especially when they were new and
their paint was still bright blue or orange or chartreuse, they
seemed no more threatening than a weed whacker or a circular
saw. But I still felt that every one of them was cunning enough to
lie in wait until it sensed the one moment out of a thousand when
its owner's attention flagged. We swore by our chain saws and
sometimes we swore at them, but we knew all the while that our
dependence on them was like nursing an asp. In all the years I
worked in the woods I never lost the feeling that disaster was just
around the corner. The chain saw becomes a perfect metaphor for
a society that lives half in love with its machines, half in fear of
them. More than once I heard one of my neighbors express the
dangers of using a chain saw in terms of a desperate technopho-
bia: "Watch yourself," Mullan said to me the first time I lifted the
saw to a log. "Them teeth don't care."

His official reason for accompanying me was to get some wood
for himself, which he always did, but unofficially I think he
wanted to make sure I didn't maim myself inadvertently, or at
least didn't maim myself without a responsible adult on hand to
drive me to the nearest medical facility, which was at least an hour
away. Still, accidents were common. They were so common, in
fact, that the emergency room staff at the Benewah Community

Hospital had much practice repairing gashes caused by sharp objects. According to local medical gossip, for anything more serious than the flu, a person should go to the hospital in Spokane. There may have been some truth to the rumor. When Nancy became pregnant with our first child in the summer of 1972, her condition was initially diagnosed in St. Maries as a hernia. She muddled through August, feeling less and less enthusiastic about nailing wallboard and splitting wood. By late September, when a physician in Moscow enlightened us as to the true reason for her malaise, our daughter was less than six months away. His news brought us great joy, and great embarrassment to boot: we had degrees from Yale University and Connecticut College, and we didn't know enough to recognize pregnancy.

If you were so unfortunate as to injure yourself with a saw, however, there was no better place than St. Maries to get stitched up. I drove Ed Strobel to town once when his saw jumped back at him and cut his upper lip in two. After they'd sewn him back together, he phoned his wife to bring her up to date. "What's it look like?" Jean asked. Strobel was annoyed by her question. "It looks like I've cut my lip with a chain saw," he answered. Yet within a month Strobel was able to talk without a lisp, and after a year's time the scar was visible only if you knew what to look for. They were wizards with a needle and some nylon.

Since chain saws are so inherently dangerous, you would think it would have been easy to find information on how to use them safely. In fact, the opposite was true. A person with a do-it-yourself bent in 1972 could find instructional manuals on just about anything from car repair to barn building. I had books on wiring, plumbing, carpentry, masonry, gardening, and animal husbandry. But as far as I was aware, there were no books on felling trees. Apart from a couple of crude cartoons in the pamphlet that came with the saw, I was on my own.

The first saw I bought was a Homelite XL with a twenty-inch cutting bar, small by professional sawyers' standards. The owner's booklet described in detail how to start and stop the saw, but little else. There was a drawing representing a man, a saw, and a tree with a notch and some vectors of force. But as for written instructions on the subject of cutting down trees, Homelite was strangely silent. You might have thought that this was knowledge a person possessed by genetic inheritance.

You saw down a large tree with the same meticulous awareness whether it's your first tree or your thousandth, and paying attention to every part of the tree from the ground up becomes part of the business of sawing. Of course you need to watch the saw and the forty or more wickedly sharp teeth whirling around the bar at better than seventy feet per second. The first time I cut down a tree on my own I felt excited and frightened. On other trips for firewood Mullan had done the felling and bucking; for my part, I was in charge of loading the trucks, a job that in the scheme of things in Alder Creek was reserved for women and adolescents. But eventually he invited me to do the sawing honors. My instinct told me to decline, but I kept my mouth shut and picked up the saw. There was no graceful way to refuse if I wanted to continue to live in this place with even a minimal amount of esteem from my neighbors. Mullan stepped back and to one side about three feet. "Watch your back cut" was his only advice.

The next few minutes were among the most intense of my life. As I remember it, I was terrified, and yet I had plenty of time on my hands to think the wildest and stupidest thoughts. If I had not been so completely convinced that I was drawing my last breaths, the whole episode would have been wonderfully comic. I was holding a brightly painted gizmo that weighed about ten or eleven pounds and with which I was expected to cause to fall to earth this thing, this *plant* for God's sake, that weighed maybe three tons and rose 120 feet above my head. I stood there dumbly in full view of three people who were waiting for me to act.

In many ways it was an act. The situation had all the elements of a stage play. I was in a space reserved for me alone, I had an audience, and I had on a costume. I wore boots, thick canvas chaps, a checkered flannel shirt (what else?), and a shiny tin helmet I had borrowed for the occasion. The helmet had no chin strap, and whenever I tipped my head back to look up at the top of the tree, the helmet fell off. I wore it with no faith in it whatever. I couldn't get out of my mind what combat soldiers sometimes said of their own helmets — that the only thing they were good for was for your buddies to scoop up your brains in case you got hit in the head.

To my surprise I discovered that felling a tree is almost a meditative experience; there are dozens of things to do and know that are invisible to the casual observer. This came as a revelation. I had expected, I suppose, a brief episode of intense emotion, a rush of excitement such as one feels in an airplane at takeoff. But it was not like that at all. Felling a tree calls for deliberation; the task has a way of insisting that you take every possible situation into account. It's a little like playing chess. This is especially true if you're felling a tree for firewood. Usually the tree has been dead for several years; it likely is missing most of its branches, and without the stabilizing effect of their mass, the trunk has little natural equilibrium. It behaves more like an upended pole than a tree, so even the smallest lateral movement can topple it. Often, as a result of years of exposure to the sun's light and heat, large cracks or "checks" in the grain extend upward thirty feet or more from the base, and these fault lines can split without warning, half the tree snapping back in the face of the sawyer.

To cut down such a thing is a labor of the mind as much as the body. You forget about the physical effort and instead listen to the senses, smell and touch and sound in addition to sight. There's a little Zen mixed with it as well. The aim is to come to full consciousness of the tree so that you can anticipate its behavior. Every time I felled a tree I was convinced I had achieved a new level of perception. It reminded me in some ways of childhood, lying in bed waiting for sleep, in tune with the smells, texture, noises, and flickering lights of the external world. The experience was distinctly preverbal. Perhaps this is why so little is written about it, and perhaps this explains in part the peculiar reticence with which real sawyers talk about their work.

What was even more uncanny was the way each tree lingered in memory. Long afterward, without maps or notes, I could find my way through miles of forest road to the exact spot where the trees I'd cut had stood; I remembered a bend in a road through the woods and a weathered snag on a mountain slope like the face of a friend. The recollection was so powerful it had to have a basis in psychology. Something about the intensity of the experience, the distinctive openness to sensation, made it unforgettable.

If felling trees is messy, dangerous, and necessarily methodical, it can sometimes become an art. It's not easy to drop a tree so that it doesn't shatter on impact, or, worse, get stuck in the branches of some neighboring trees halfway down. Bill McPherson once told me about the time when he first logged the area around Alder Creek just after World War I. "The hardest part was finding the first tree to fall," he said. "Them trees was spaced so evenly there wasn't no room anywhere to drop one. It took me all morning to find an opening to lay down the first tree."

The way a person fells a tree leaves considerable room for individual choice; occasionally, in exercising these preferences individual sawyers develop their own personal styles. There are different ways to notch trees, different ways to handle the saw on the back cut, different felling techniques for different saws or for different types of trees or for different conditions. I was taught, for example, to make the second, or slant, cut on my notch on the top; since about the mid 1970s, however, professional sawyers have been using the Humboldt cut, which puts the slant cut of the felling notch on the bottom, toward the stump. This saves about half a foot or so of wood. And really skilled sawyers can vary their cutting so as to bring the tree down exactly where they want in the manner they want. One of the rarest maneuvers is the Flying Dutchman. This is so difficult and so seldom used that even a professional forester I talked to had yet to see it performed. Paul Robnett, a forester who worked for Pacific Crown in Plummer, one of the towns within the Coeur d'Alene tribal reservation, told me about the Flying Dutchman one day as we cruised some timber by my south fence line.

"You use it if you wanted to get some timber that was leaning a little ways over a fence line," he said. "The trick is to get the tree to fall away from where it's leaning toward the fence. You make your notch on the fence side and then instead of a regular back cut you sort of spiral the nose of the saw from one side to the other so that when the tree starts to fall it spins and breaks loose and kind of jumps off the stump. If you do it right, when the butt hits the ground it jerks the top right back so's it falls in the other direction."

It sounds impossible, but Robnett assured me that though he personally hadn't seen this done, he knew a couple of sawyers who could do it maybe three out of five tries. What a marvel of achievement! In a perfectly egalitarian world, maybe the people who can defy physics in that way ought to be celebrated right up there with Nancy Kerrigan's triple axel or Michael Jordan's hang time. As for me, the Flying Dutchman belongs with the sun's legendary green flash in the Tropics as among the several phenomena I most want to witness.

My career as a weekend logger was not without mishaps. The last time I got firewood with Mullan was also very nearly the last time he did anything on earth. All through the summers of 1973 and 1974, Nancy and I got firewood each weekend with him and his family. It was a chance to socialize while doing backbreaking work, but more important, because Mullan worked for Potlatch his presence on firewood expeditions seemed the next best thing to a woods permit. We loaded the trucks and rode out at about six in the morning when the sun was just beginning to warm up, and we were back well before noon.

On this particular morning, I decided to fell the tree by myself. Mullan remained by the trucks. The tree, a large tamarack snag, stood maybe seventy-five feet off the road, towering over anything nearby. The bottom twenty feet were obscured by the undergrowth, and by the time I reached the base I lost sight of trucks and people. I heard footfalls and distant voices but nothing intelligible, and then the only things on my mind were the saw and the tree.

Five minutes, maybe ten. The saw threw a rooster tail of chips against my thigh. I felt them but didn't really see them; it was a constant hydraulic pressure, like sticking your hand into the current of a stream. Then absolute silence. I strained against the glare of the sun to see the top of the tree leaning out against the empty sky. It was a moment of pure leisure, as if time had stopped. The pleasure was almost narcotic. Winston Churchill once mused that there was nothing so exhilarating as being shot at and missed. For a novice like me, seeing that several tons of tree by some miracle was falling in the opposite direction was similarly thrilling. Then the tree was down. I slipped the wedge back into my pocket, gathered up the maul and the saw, and walked happily through the brush toward the road.

As I came out of the brush I heard Nancy shouting. At first I couldn't make out what she was saying. Later she told me that what she was shouting was "You killed him! You killed him!" But my hearing was still recovering from the noise of the saw, and so until I got to the road and could actually see her, I didn't understand her.

This is what had happened while I was felling the tree. During the time I took to clear the debris from around the base and make the front cut, Mullan left his position by the trucks and began to wander up the road. Nancy saw him walking on the road, and she knew I couldn't see him. But she also knew that he was competent to look after himself in the woods. Hadn't Mullan taught her husband everything he knew about felling a tree? So she assumed he wanted merely to get a closer look before the tree came down. Worse, she assumed that Mullan could tell well in advance, as she could not, what was happening by the sound of the saw. Still worse, she didn't know that at 8:15 A.M. Mullan was already groggy from the coffee and vodka he'd been drinking for two hours. The truth was that Mullan had no idea what was about to happen, and he certainly couldn't tell when or where the tree would fall. So he stood still, grinning, watching the road and the woods and now and then the huge tamarack.

Then the sawing stopped, and — as Nancy told it — a great many things happened suddenly and at once. The tree leaned out and out toward the road. Then it started down, and Mullan, who at that point still must have considered himself an interested observer, stiffened with awareness. It was coming right at him. Just as the tree seemed to be on top of him, he hurled himself outward. His leap and the crash of the tree were so close together they seemed part of the same event, and Nancy could not tell whether

Mullan had leaped of his own will or had been struck and sent fly-
ing like a ball off a bat. The topmost thirty feet of the tree smashed
across the road, and as it hit the ground it threw up an explosion
of dust that obliterated man, tree, and road from sight. It was at
that moment back in the woods that I had pocketed the wedge
and started to walk toward the road and had heard my wife's
screams. She was still screaming hysterically at me when I shuffled
smugly out onto the road. Before I could make out what she was
saying, the dust cleared and I saw Mullan walking from the spot
where the tree lay. On his face was a look of complete amazement.
Jonah must have looked like that when he emerged from the belly
of the whale.

   Mullan didn't say a word. He opened the gate of his truck and
climbed into the bed and lay down. Within minutes he was asleep.
The vodka belatedly took effect, and soon he was snoring loudly.
By that time it had sunk in what had nearly happened, and both
Nancy and I were giddy with relief. We looked around us at the
wood and the snoozing woodsman. If anybody asks, she said, we'll
tell them our wood permit is asleep in the back of the truck. We
loaded both trucks; I drove Mullan's truck and Nancy ours. When
we got back we offloaded Mullan and his wood in his driveway,
where, his wife told us later, he slept for the rest of the morning.

7

Hay for the Horses

It's late July 1972. The house and goat shed are full of visitors from New York, eager to experience "country life." Partly to accommodate them, and partly to show our own willingness to join the community, we agree to help Fred Rainbolt get his winter's hay.

Fred was a Native American, the first I had ever met. In the late sixties, he and his wife, Nina, had retired to the Idaho panhandle from southern California. They took out a mortgage on several hundred acres where the Alder Creek Road dead-ended at the Benewah Road, the main road to town. Rainbolt always had an eye for a bargain, and he took advantage of rising property values, selling a forty-acre parcel each year to make the next payment on his balloon mortgage, until in the end he wound up with a forty-acre piece paid for by the profits he'd made selling all the others. In exchange for helping Fred lay up hay for his small herd of beef cows, he offered us a truckload of recycled cedar siding he'd obtained when he tore down an old mink farm. It seemed like a surprisingly good deal: a thousand board feet of cedar for two days' labor.

A meadow strewn with bales of hay is as lovely as poetry. Before the grass is baled it must dry for at least several days. It lies across the field in neat little windrows, and as it dries it turns from green to a luminous gold. As the grass takes on a new color it takes on a new scent as well — dried, it is sweeter, more delicate, and surprisingly sensual. The change in the grass is great enough to seem a metamorphosis, and in fact that's what its new name signifies: once it is dried, grass is no longer grass, but hay.

It's a humbling sight, especially at evening. Light, field, sky: it's nature made into art, color and light and pale high blue sky, all faintly glowing. The western sky at close of day seems almost impossibly remote. This is the "big sky" celebrated in A. B. Guthrie's novel and advertised beneath a stylized rim of mountains on Montana's license plates. The phenomenon is real — the Montana sky is indeed bigger than the sky of New Jersey, although the apparent size of the western sky is due more to an accident of climate than to terrestrial features. The air in summer in the West is almost never sufficiently laden with moisture to lower the dome of the sky to familiar reaches.

Hayfields are as old as agriculture, but only the last few generations of human eyes have seen sights such as this. It is odd that the blunt regularity of the mechanically created bales adds to the picturesque effect. Hundreds of parallelepipeds strewn over the field force geometry on nature. The whole scene is artistically satisfying, like the patterns on a tiled floor. Yet not perfectly so: at the same time, the curving contours of the field, the rise and dip of the land, along with the irregularity of the bales' orientations — they bounce randomly upon being ejected from the baler and so point in various directions — are sufficiently chaotic to prevent the scene from being read as a design. Your eye scans the field simultaneously for these two pictorial values, randomness and order.

Of course I am joking. Yet it was impossible to scan the field and not sense its openness to symbolic meaning. Now and then a lone bale, because of some quirk of density, momentum, or terrain, will teeter for a few seconds and remain standing on end. Like photographs that capture their subjects in sadly vulnerable moments, these upright bales hold your attention. Roland Barthes calls such details in photographs the *punctum* — an accidental presence (literally, a prick or wound) that transcends the rest of the scene and makes it real.

But working in a hayfield belied its pastoral loveliness. "Pastoral" is a misleading term, implying some lazy summer idyll. In reality, the job involved moving countless bulky, prickly objects to and fro in the summer heat, and the work proceeded with bleak monotony. Ranches in the Benewah Valley and along Alder Creek lacked the expensive machinery needed to make the huge biscuit-like rolls of grass that are moved entirely by forklift or tractor. In Alder Creek, hay was made the old-fashioned way, with muscle and Depression-era machinery.

Say you have a small herd of beef cattle, maybe six or eight Angus or Hereford steers and a couple of cows for breeding. From a neighbor who keeps some of his land in grass you arrange to buy a certain amount of hay — say, to be generous (for you don't want to run out of hay two weeks before the grass greens in May), two tons per animal per season. You make your contract in May or early June, when the character of the growing season and the quality of the grass have been established. The grass has got an early start this year; Jim Yearout has eighty acres of good creek bottomland, which he has sowed with alfalfa seed to improve the quality of his hay. Better for the livestock, but of course improved quality of product means you pay a higher price. The going rate for alfalfa, as advertised by word of mouth and by occasional advertisements in the *St. Maries Gazette Record,* is $25 a ton. In the summer of 1972, $500 buys twenty tons of hay, cut, dried, raked, and baled, ready to fetch from Jim Yearout's field on the Alder Creek Loop Road. Would we, Fred Rainbolt asked, help him get in his hay?

We did. This is how it went. My job was to walk behind the truck as it motored slowly back and forth through the field, pick up the bales, and load them. It was simple physical labor, but it was impossible to find a comfortable pace. From a distance the bales looked spaced in orderly rows, but actually they were scattered irregularly enough to upset any work rhythm. Sometimes a half-dozen bales lay bunched together in the field, and I would have to rush to load them so the truck didn't have to stop. Other times, in places where for some reason the grass grew thinner or where the baling machine had temporarily jammed, the bales were widely scattered; here Rainbolt sped up and I had to trot to keep up.

I worked all day in full sun, and the unremitting light and heat made my actions lethargic and dull. The work became mindless ritual. I understood what Bertrand Russell meant when he said that there were really only two kinds of jobs, moving things from one place to another and telling somebody to move things from one place to another. For a time I envied Rainbolt in the cab of the truck — even if it wasn't air conditioned, at least he was in the shade. But there were times when the truck was almost fully loaded that he nearly tipped over traveling across a slope, and eventually I came to believe I had the better part of the bargain. I might be worked to death, but at least I wouldn't suffer the indignity of being buried under a truckload of hay.

The action each time was the same: bend, grasp the bale by the wires, one in each hand, and in a continuous motion something like a weightlifter's press-and-jerk, heave it onto the bed of the truck. After I'd thrown up five or six bales I swung on board and stacked them. On the flatbed I piled the bales like bricks, overlapping each of them by half and always facing them nap to nap. ("Don't set bales on the sides," Fred told me. "They'll slip right off one another.") For the pickup I first filled the bed to the height of the sides, then laid pairs of bales crossways back to front so that at least a foot hung over each side. Angled down slightly from the sides to the center of the truck bed, these bales formed a shallow trough that stabilized the remaining four or five layers on top. It sounded flimsy when Rainbolt described it to me, but in practice it proved surprisingly stable. The crosswise bales directed all the weight of the uppermost layers toward the inside and toward each other, like an upside-down corbel.

The bales looked inert, but they were not. Even when I tried to be careful, a bale would often bow or curl as I hoisted it into the truck. Sometimes I wasn't quick enough to catch it, and it twisted and disassembled into a sorry and useless pile of loose flakes. A broken bale, like a broken egg, can't ever be put together again.

There was nothing to do but let it lie in the field, and for days afterward, visible to everyone who passed by, my greenhorn mistakes lay strewn around Yearout's meadow.

By late morning of the first day, I faced up to the wearying monotony that was in store for the next day and a half. In the sun and the thin dry air the smell of the grass soon grew oppressive. After three long hours working in the open field, it actually cleared my head to linger close behind the truck and inhale the smells of unburnt gas and overworked clutch lining. Time stretched ahead of me, farther than I could imagine. I felt captive; it was like being a kid in school again, yearning for summer. We worked in heat and dust past midday and through the long slow hours of late afternoon. I got some insight into what it must be like to be a beast of burden. My mind shut down to take in only the most elemental things: the evening haze and the insects' buzz and an increasingly desperate lust for a cataract of beer.

At some point it dawned on me, the mindlessness of what I was doing. It was a grim vision: one bale at a time — say, an average of seventy-five pounds — lift it up to the truck, then lift it again to stack it so it won't fall off as the truck lurches drunkenly across a hidden wash or gopher hole, then lift it a third time, heaving it in the dust before the barn, and then, when the truck is empty, dismount and lift each bale once more to stagger up my own private ziggurat. At some point, as I say, it dawned on me that from sunrise to sundown I was personally responsible for the translocation of better than ninety thousand pounds of matter that within the space of half a year was all going to be expelled from a cow's asshole.

It was a sobering thought. That was the tough-minded truth about getting in hay, the grim necessity of repetition. You lift bales from the ground onto a truck so you can drive them to a distant site where you lift them again to place them on the ground so that you can lift them a third time to stack them in a barn where they will remain for three or four months when for the fourth and last time they will be lifted (blessedly, by someone else) to move them to the ground to be eaten. It's a massive deployment of mind and muscle solely for the purpose of shuffling forty-five tons of matter as prelude to its becoming mostly shit.

As if in keeping with its deadening repetitiveness, the work proceeded without socialization. We didn't talk, we didn't goof off; the work was cumbersome, but the pace was slightly frantic, like the action in a silent film. We labored under the constant pressure of time. Make a load, drive to the barn, offload and stack the bales in the barn, ten minutes for water and a piss (more repetitiveness: fluids in, fluids out), and then back to the field. By late morning we'd completed one trip. We worked through lunch, eating sandwiches on the return trip to the field, completed another trip by midafternoon, and returned for the third and last load of the day. The next day was just like the first. After that, Rainbolt said, it could rain all it wanted.

It was an odd thing to say; there wasn't a cloud in the sky. Yet it was clear proof of how powerfully myth and lore shape human behavior. Perhaps it's not surprising that a mood of urgency should attend the annual ritual of getting in hay. The economy of laying in hay allows you to feed all your animals with two or three days' hard work, but they have to be the right two or three days. Choose wrong, and suddenly you're facing a crisis. For a farmer whose future depends on the grass that's lying in the field, rain at the wrong time is far more than an inconvenience; it may mean an irrecoverable loss. To think of getting in hay is to weigh the possibilities of rain, and there is a point at which every farmer's conversation about hay turns to the weather. The trick, as everybody knows, is to make hay while the sun shines. This is valid, if not particularly shrewd, advice for farmers in upland Virginia or the plains of Salisbury, but it's a remarkably irrelevant piece of information for someone in Alder Creek, where it rarely rains in August. Yet we acted out what our culture had taught us about agriculture; I felt like the cloddish farmer in Frost's famous poem about two men who maintained a useless wall simply because "good fences make good neighbors."

That fall, in school and studying literature, I discovered a poem about haying by Gary Snyder called "Hay for the Horses." Snyder tells the story of an old man who drives through the night down

mountain roads on the northern Pacific coast to deliver a truck-
load of hay to a large California ranch:

> He had driven half the night
> From far down San Joaquin
> Through Mariposa, up the
> Dangerous mountain roads,
> And pulled in at eight A.M.,
> With his big truckload of hay
>   behind the barn.
> With winch and ropes and hooks
> We stacked the bales up clean
> To splintery redwood rafters
> High in the dark, flecks of alfalfa
> Whirling through shingle-cracks of light,
> Itch of haydust in the
>   sweaty shirt and shoes.
> At lunchtime under Black oak
> Out in the hot corral,
> — The old mare nosing lunchpails,
> Grasshoppers crackling in the weeds —
> "I'm sixty-eight" he said,
> "I first bucked hay when I was seventeen.
> I thought, that day I started,
> I sure would hate to do this all my life.
> And dammit, that's just what
> I've gone and done."

If life really is a journey toward self-understanding, it's proba-
bly more like Snyder's poem than the searing revelations of Greek
tragedy. But Snyder must have seen, in the simple, callous neces-
sity of everyday life, the literary qualities of irrevocableness and
ironic enlightenment: "Dammit," I can imagine Oedipus saying as
he recollects the words of the oracle, "that's just what I've gone
and done."

Nothing about haying seemed rational. From one angle it was
a backbreaking shuffling of matter from one place to another;
at the same time the work was blunt, necessary, elemental. It
wasn't the least bit glamorous or romantic. I would never say that

I found it confirming and pleasurable, and I would not grant that its monotonous rhythms had mythic force. But it always set my imagination traveling: the animal, the grass, the barn, and the history of agriculture and poetry as well, all in a nutshell. It was an insight such as I'd never got in a classroom, plain enough even for a first-year graduate student.

8

Builders, Buildings, and Build-Ons

SOONER OR LATER if you own a house you will wish that it were different or that it were bigger. Probably both. Wanting someplace different or bigger to live in is a desire as irrational as it is common. For these reasons the pharaohs built pyramids and Louis XIV built Versailles. The same yearnings, transplanted to America in the late twentieth century, give Bob Vila a loyal audience for his televised renovations of old houses.

Setting aside the question of the source of this so-called edifice complex, I don't think the people in Alder Creek were any different from anyone else. On the other hand, I have never seen people who showed less pride in their dwellings than my neighbors did. Your first impression of the homesteads along the Benewah might be contempt. Most of the houses looked downright shabby.

The houses looked a little run-down because their occupants were always tinkering with them. Houses in Alder Creek were like Web sites, perpetually under construction. Russell Gore's house stood waiting for siding for thirty years, covered temporarily with tarpaper and battens. For nearly as long, the front door of another native opened onto a vertical drop of four feet. There were always needs more pressing, apparently, than a front stoop. Economics was a factor, of course; so were skill and time. Sometimes, though, it wasn't lack of money or skills or time that kept these houses from being completed. In Alder Creek, a front door to nowhere was not generally taken to be a sign of incompleteness, much less personal failure. In a peculiar way, to have your house unfinished could stand as proof of your long-term housing aspirations. Almost everybody I knew who lived in Alder Creek lived in a house that they believed, deep in their hearts, was not the Big House they would someday build. So the walls were particle board and the drawer pulls nonexistent, so family and friends always used the back door, but so what? These were flaws that didn't trouble us because we knew that the Big House would come later.

It's a strange take on oneself and the world, the belief that non-completion is itself a state of completeness — as if God, late on the evening of the sixth day, had hung out a sign, "In Process." The interesting thing was how believing in the dream of the Big House made it so easy to settle for second best. You could live your life without using the front door because you knew that it was only temporary.

Not that my neighbors and I weren't aware that our carelessness was seriously flawed. We assessed our guilt pretty accurately, and we developed an ironic stance with which to frame it. Whenever we got to the point in a project where a thing was functional, if not finished, we'd set down our tools and say, "A fellow could live like that for years." And usually we did. As a philosophy, it was a late variety of pragmatism. If a door or a window would open and close, however awkwardly, if a car would run or a fence stand up, however haltingly, we were finished.

In other ages similar attitudes might have fallen under the scrutiny of moralists and theologians. It would have been hard for the generations of workers who built the cathedrals of Chartres and Rouen to accommodate themselves to anything that fell short of their ideals. My neighbors and I, on the other hand, were always able to subordinate perfection to utility. It's easier to hang a curtain than a door in the entrance to the bathroom, easier still to train the eye not to see the bare nailheads in the Sheetrock. What is at first an inconvenience or an eyesore soon becomes tolerable, then acceptable, eventually normal.

Once I was helping Bill Fletcher restring some wire along a fence. We kicked some of the posts to align them, hooked a claw hammer through the wire to lever it tighter, and drove in a couple of staples here and there to hold it snug. It wasn't perfect, and it sure wasn't pretty, but it looked like it would deter the cows for a couple of weeks at least.

"That's good enough for the Benewah," Fletcher said.

With that we laughed and quit work.

Fletcher's remark came to stand as a kind of credo for the way we were. Often repeated, it eventually passed into local idiom: "That's good enough for the Benewah."

In spite of some obvious shortcomings, the dwellings in Alder Creek had a certain overall coherence. The terminology for a good deal of the housing activity was peculiar and local. If you live in the city or suburbs and take your ideas for expanding your house to a contractor, you'll talk about building an "addition" or an "annex." In Alder Creek, however, you enlarged your house by constructing what was called a "build-on." There were build-ons and there were Build-Ons. If one were to write a psychosocial history of Alder Creek, a good place to start would be to study all the construction projects begun and ultimately left incomplete: Orville Pierson's concrete block foundation, built in the shape of a pentagon; Doug and Lisa Fawcett's dream house, two and a half stories of superbly crafted timber-and-frame that only Doug himself, an itinerant painter, lived in on weekends after Lisa and the two little girls moved out; the Belkos' basement, covered with empty cans; the pair of root cellars Mullan and I built one summer to pass the time when the woods were closed by drought; and a dozen or so lean-tos and frame shells scattered here and there in the woods by their makers — Reynolds, Harris, Robinette, Garay, and Comstock.

Abandoned, these unfinished bits of architecture are abiding proof of the way individuality imprints itself onto matter. These buildings and parts of buildings are labor turned into artifact. They still carry the fingerprints of their makers, and they announce the peculiar dreams and the agony of those makers as eloquently as the group signatures on the casing blocks of the Meidum pyramid: "Boat Gang," "South Gang," "Enduring Gang,"

"Vigorous Gang." None of the works is so melancholy to me, how-
ever, as the simple extra room Ed Strobel built on to the northwest
side of his house.

Ed and Jean Strobel had a place on the Alder Creek Loop Road,
a four-mile-long detour that took off from the main road just
west of our place, meandered for a while along Alder Creek, even-
tually rejoining the county road at the Brede ranch. Since most of
the population was clustered along this bypass, even though it was
a lesser road it bore most of the traffic.

Ed and Jean were both in their mid-fifties. They looked like a
local version of the couple in Grant Wood's famous painting
American Gothic. Strobel normally dressed in coveralls and a flan-
nel shirt, and unless Jean was going to town she wore a housecoat
and bedroom slippers. The day we met them, Strobel was recov-
ering from a back injury he'd sustained while helping Lowell
Radke break a horse to saddle. He was genial but shy about speak-
ing his mind, a natural bias that had been encouraged, perhaps, by
a career spent as an enlisted seaman. As for Jean, you sensed that
she had once been vivacious, but she was being worn down from
worry over the fortunes of her children and her own failing
health.

Strobel was a skilled craftsman, patient with materials almost
to the point of reverence. His meticulous habits were out of keep-
ing with the half-assed workmanship that was the norm with me
and my neighbors; with his coveralls and toolbox, he could have
walked in and out of the courts of fabled Byzantium. He spent a
week combing the woods for the right piece of vine maple to use
for an ax handle; he labored slowly for many months just to join
a single small room and loft to the northwest side of his house.

Like everything else he did in life, Strobel undertook this proj-
ect with precision. The old house was first squared up on its foun-
dation, the back sill replaced to give the new room a level orienta-
tion. Day after day Strobel carefully fitted joists, plumbed walls,
planed trim boards. He brought to its making a superlative degree
of craftsmanship and dedication, and all the while he was work-
ing, he was building, as it turned out, the room in which his wife
would one day take her life. One night a few days before they were

to leave to retire to Arizona, Jean covered her head with a plastic trash bag, opened the valve on a propane tank, and asphyxiated. None of us had seen it coming. Jean's suicide caused an emptiness that was impossible to fill. It was difficult to fathom an irony so cruel; that Strobel's artistry should have been a key element in his personal tragedy made the world seem mysterious and very dangerous.

By far the most common build-on consisted of an addition to a mobile home. The simplest structural improvement you could make to such a home was to enclose it in an open frame with a gable roof. The idea seems suspiciously redundant; why would you buy a mobile home in the first place if you wanted to surround it with a permanent building? Yet they were very popular, and there were three or four such combinations built in Alder Creek or along the Benewah Valley. It was hard to get used to them. They always looked incongruous, a simple pole frame that supported a gable roof perched oddly over glass, vinyl, and aluminum. It was axmanship and the assembly line in a single image.

There was method in this architectural madness. Mobile homes were cheap and handy, but they had flat roofs, and in the long Idaho winters those roofs were notorious for developing leaks. The idea was at least to protect the original roof from the weather, and so their owners built pole frames around three sides of the mobile home to support a steeply pitched roof to shed the ice and snow.

This was what Kenny and Beverly Mullan did. They had bought the forty acres across the road from our place intending to transform the raw land into a prosperous homestead. But their chances of building the lives they imagined for themselves were slim. Most of the land was too high to farm and too far from town for daily commuting. I have never seen anyone work harder than Mullan for the first four or five years he lived in Alder Creek. But the harder he worked, the more he wore himself down. In the end, in large part the result of too much time on the road and not enough time to recover his wilted spirits, he ceased trying, having worked himself into a state of dullness.

Alder Creek was really an idler's kind of place. Only two types of people stood a chance of making a reasonable life for themselves here, large landowners or retirees. If you owned a lot of land — I once figured it would take about a section, or 640 acres — you could sell enough timber annually from one of your forties to get the modest cash income you needed. By the time you logged your last forty, sixteen years later, the first would be ready for another cutting. In this way you might escape the trap of driving to St. Maries, Plummer, or Coeur d'Alene to earn a paycheck. When we lived in Alder Creek there were still a few families who could do that.

The other way to stay in Alder Creek was to retire there with a fat pension check; we had neighbors who had been navy pilots or Los Angeles cops. With a good pension you could spend your days fussing with local projects, knowing that your checks were in the mail. There was really no other choice, unless you were one of the few people who didn't care to have an income in the first place.

At that time the Mullan place was undeveloped, as they say in the real estate business. Electric and telephone lines ran by it along the road; otherwise, the place had been untouched since it was logged half a century earlier. I mention this to give some idea of the huge challenge that Mullan faced in establishing a working household on his property. It is no trouble at all to make oneself comfortable for a night or even a week in the woods. You don't need much equipment — a bedroll, some cooking gear, and a sack of food. All the rest of life and life's necessities get suspended; you just live temporarily off momentum. It is infinitely harder if you are trying to make a permanent home out of nothing. At least the colonists in Massachusetts and Virginia had each other's company, but for a single family trying to homestead, there's so much to do it's terrifying.

From the start Mullan was besieged with the myriad of projects necessary to turn forty empty acres into a place where people could live. He was like the man shipwrecked on an island in A. A. Milne's poem "The Old Sailor," forever unable to begin a task, whether making a boat or a dwelling or a sun hat or a fence, because there was always something else that needed to be done first. In the end, Milne's sailor does nothing but bask on the beach until one day he is saved. But you can't bask in the north Idaho sun much past the first of September.

It makes you sort through your priorities, homesteading. What's most important? Water? But what's the point of drilling a well if you lack electricity to pump the water from 350 feet below the surface? So perhaps it would be best to have the power installed to pump water and run power tools. But should you spend time putting in electricity now, in May, when you had better use the small window of opportunity to plant a garden? But how can you plant before you fence out Brede's cows? Maybe the garden should be postponed. You can shop for vegetables at Safeway in November, all right, but would there be a roof over your head by then? Perhaps it was best to start the house so you had a place to live come winter.

These are the kinds of decisions no one any longer teaches us to make. We lack our ancestors' genius for organization, not to mention their willingness to endure meager rations and miserable conditions. And we lack their easy familiarity with real things, a familiarity they acquired as children as a matter of course.

So Mullan did the only practical thing he could. He bought a secondhand mobile home and had it hauled onto a site on his land. Now he had instant shelter, electricity, phone, and heat. All he had to do was find a way to get water into his house, and then make arrangements for getting it back out. He dug a well, installed a pump and dug a water line to the house site, put in a septic tank and a drain field, and then set about making his home his castle. Which meant a build-on.

The architectural principles of Mullan's build-on were common throughout Alder Creek. You build a shell to embrace an existing mobile home. So far as I could tell, he built it entirely by instinct. Benewah County had not yet adopted a building code, and Mullan's only plan was to build in multiples of four and eight feet so as to use basic materials of the building industry to greatest advantage. Walls, joists, even rafters were constructed of two-by-fours he'd bought as culls — what people outside the industry would call rejects — from a local mill. Much of this lumber was bowed or knotty. It could be used safely only wherever it did not have to bear much load, and as a result Mullan had to cull the culls before he could erect his walls, floor, and roof.

In turn, roof and wall sheathing, flooring and subflooring (no one in Alder Creek made any distinction) were made of technically substandard sheets of half-inch exterior-grade plywood, known locally as "blows." These sheets were cut slightly off square or had begun to delaminate, defects that made them unsuitable for commercial use but good enough for builders and buildings in Alder Creek.

As was often the case with Mullan, the project was conceived on a grand scale. It dwarfed the mobile home it was in theory constructed to supplement. The ridge line peaked a good fifteen feet above the flat roof. At the front end the ridge hung several feet over the limit of the mobile home, but at the back end it stretched beyond by nearly twenty feet. Measured in the other direction, Mullan's build-on more than tripled the width of the structure it enclosed, creating behind it and beyond it a huge L-shaped space.

This space Mullan divided into three big rooms, the walls framed and covered with more culls and more blows. Above, in a space never even crudely finished, were to be two more rooms. The work proceeded for most of a year. Mullan installed insulation, metal roofing, and a door. I wired the build-on for him in exchange for some labor I've long since forgotten — probably mechanicking. But before the space actually became habitable, during the period in which the excitement of erecting a structure yields to the tedious reality of finish carpentry, work on the expansion flagged, then ceased. That winter the space slowly became a cold storage facility for tools, feed, and machinery.

Two years later Mullan, having bought thirty acres that adjoined his land, moved into the house on the new property. The house that came with the place was brand-new but modest. It had been built as a retirement house, and it had a living room, kitchen, and two bedrooms. It was much too small for a family of seven, and so immediately Mullan set about enlarging it.

The first build-on, I now saw, was merely a warmup exercise. The new one was gargantuan. Its nearest architectural relative was the airplane hangar. The kids were growing up; the older two boys were already in high school. Mullan's job was steady and paid well. It was time now for the dream house, the Big House.

And it was *big*. It extended out from two sides of the original house, ten feet to the rear and twenty feet on one side, and it rose above the existing structure by a full story. There were four new bedrooms upstairs and a new master bedroom downstairs, a double garage, a crafts room, a balcony, a mud room, a laundry room, a foyer, and a walk-in meat locker big enough to hang a small herd of carcasses. Fifteen rooms in all, not counting hallways, the double garage, and the meat locker. And over the entire structure, embracing new and old carpentry under a single peaked roof, stretched unbroken nearly seventy feet of shining tin.

I have never seen anything like it, before or since. It isn't easy for humans to register the presence of themselves and the things they build against the western landscape, but this building was different. It towered, it sprawled. As you drove west over the crest of the hill, it took you by surprise. The effect was dramatic even if you were prepared for it. The place looked like a cottage on steroids. Relying on experience and traditional lines, Mullan had made the big house very much like a small house. It made you feel that you were a Lilliputian getting your first glimpse of Gulliver.

To frame up the new house was difficult enough; to roof it was an amazing feat for one man; to complete it would have been the labor of a lifetime. Mullan undertook a task for which there was neither world nor time enough. Work proceeded furiously until about the stage when it was ready for the finish carpentry, and there it ceased. Unpainted Sheetrock covered the walls, plywood subflooring functioned as main flooring, wires ran exposed to fixtures and junction boxes. The Mullans moved into the house in the summer of 1977, with the kids ranging in age from five to fifteen, and then over the next fifteen years, one by one, they left. Then Kenny moved out, first to a camper shell he installed behind the house, next to the woodshed, and ultimately, after the divorce, to Homer, Alaska. Beverly lived on alone in the house until 1995, but her heart wasn't in it and in the end she occupied only three of the fifteen rooms, the rest having gone over to flies and mice.

The next year we bought the land and house from her and Kenny and set about restoring the downstairs part to rent out. We saw Beverly frequently after that, but always in her new town environment. We remained good friends, but she refused to return to Alder Creek to visit. It wasn't that she remembered her life there with bitterness or nostalgia; it was the thought of seeing the house again that kept her away. Seeing it brought her to a state of bleak fatalism, as if she were looking at an old photograph of herself and remembering vain childhood dreams.

"I can't stand to see work being done on the house" was what she said.

9

Scrounging

MID-JANUARY 1975. The road to Avery is treacherous, glazed
with melting ice. But it seems as if half the population of Alder
Creek is traveling that road along the St. Joe River today, not once
but four, five, half a dozen times. We're risking life and limb to
make the trip forty miles upriver to take advantage of an unex-
pected windfall. Up in Avery a boxcar loaded with barley has de-
railed and spilled half its contents on the main line. Traffic is
blocked while the line is being cleared, and the Chicago, Milwau-
kee, and St. Paul Railroad, in a magnificent gesture that combines
practical economics with public relations, is offering to sell the
grain at a dollar a bag to whoever wants to haul it away. We hear
the news from Kenny Mullan, who heard it from Lowell Radke,
who heard it from Russell Gore. We swarm over the barley like a
plague of locusts. By the time I get under way, Radke is on his sec-
ond bottle and his third trip.

We need the barley to feed our animals. Like every one of our
neighbors, we kept livestock. It was a small operation, just one Jer-
sey calf and a sow that we had bought from Radke on assurance
that she was pregnant. (The impregnation in fact occurred only
after money had changed hands; what we had really bought, we
learned later, was a sow and a session with a boar.) For someone
who was used to measuring animal feed in cupfuls of Kitty Chow,
the appetites of two very large ungulates, one growing and the
other growing a litter, was staggering to comprehend. A sack of
grain I could scarcely lift disappeared within days. It began to

seem as if I owed my paycheck to the Purina Feed Store in Moscow, and that was how Nancy, our young daughter, and I came to find ourselves driving along with our neighbors in a loose convoy of vehicles upriver to Avery.

The St. Joe had not yet been designated by act of Congress a "wild and scenic river," and so the river and its environs really were wild and scenic then, because few people had a mind to travel a road that federal funds had not first paved. The road alongside the St. Joe River was "seasonal," as Rand McNally described it, and in the winter it was little used. And not without reason: the asphalt ceased about ten miles east of St. Maries, and for the remaining thirty-odd miles to Avery the road was dirt — narrow, high, and full of blind curves. Worst of all, in early morning or late afternoon the direction of travel was aligned with the rising or setting sun. When the sun shone at low angles across a snowy landscape onto a windshield smeared with road salt and washer fluid, all you could do was look out the side window and navigate by maintaining a safe distance from the edge of the road. You moved forward in the hopeful sideways attitude of a crab.

The boxcar had derailed and burst on the main line at the eastern end of the town, and the railroad was taking a substantial loss just to clear the tracks. When we got to town I recognized many of my neighbors: Mullan, Bill and Esta Fletcher, and of course Radke. Radke, I learned, had nearly come to disaster. Drowsy from alcohol, he decided to take a nap in the cab of his truck. But he parked his little yellow Datsun a couple of feet too close to the tracks, and when a Milwaukee freight came through the locomotive snagged the rear bumper of the truck and spun it violently around. "Jesus, Bill," Radke exclaimed, "it woke me right up."

All that day we drove back and forth over icy roads to collect that dollar-a-bag barley. I made two trips and saved maybe fifty or sixty dollars in grain — scarcely worth it even for somebody whose farming budget was as impoverished as mine. It was the most dangerous driving I've ever done; besides the risk to life and property, the time spent and the money saved by the expedition were grossly out of balance.

So why did we do it? There was the thrill of getting something for nothing, or almost nothing. But the real lure of the escapade lay deeper. Although none of us would have confessed it, I think we did it for the pleasure of each other's company. An occasion like the barley expedition was never structured formally like the quilting bees or barn raisings of America's colonial days, but I think it served much the same social purpose.

The economic savings to be had in a joint enterprise were merely an excuse; more often than not my neighbors and I joined in projects whose need was marginal or nonexistent. One summer when woods operations were shut down because of drought, Mullan and I happened to have the loan of a backhoe. There's nothing more likely to cause mischief than a couple of idle men in charge of some large earth-moving equipment, and for two weeks we dug a series a large holes in the ground. We said we were building root cellars, which was true, although at the time we didn't have ten pounds of produce to store in them. Even then, I knew that the real point was not economic but social. It was a ritual enactment of harmony between native and newcomer, as the cultural anthropologists might put it.

The Idaho woods provided my neighbors and me many opportunities for collective scrounging. As far as Eino Jacobsen was concerned, the forest was a communist enterprise, and he took great pleasure in gathering and stockpiling different kinds of wood he thought one day might be useful. Jacobsen had landed in Alder Creek after several aborted careers, in New Hampshire in secondary education and then in the silver mines of north Idaho, and he built a small cabin on the bluffs overlooking the lower reaches of the creek. He was a skilled carpenter — carpentry was another of his careers — and was passionate about collecting wood for future building projects, especially cedar. Jacobsen dreamed of a plan to float hundreds of bolts of cedar down Alder Creek to Frank Burger's ranch. Like many of my neighbors' schemes — one wanted to haul salmon from Alaska on a bed of ice in a pickup truck, another began to build an airplane in his basement, then had to build a garage to accommodate construction once the wings were attached — Jacobsen's vision was elemental, grand,

and bold. It was the kind of dream that thrives in the West. More than once he laid out his plan to me.

"Hell, Bill," he said with characteristic enthusiasm, "there's enough cedar down there to shake every roof in Coeur d'Alene."

The trees he talked about were long dead and long down. Most of them had been felled when the country was first logged, early in the century. Loggers then had little interest in anything other than north Idaho's huge white pines; the cedars were cut down only because they were in the way. Then they were left behind. In time the skid trails grew shut, and the cedar suffered little harm for nearly half a century, inaccessible by vehicle and immune, by virtue of the resin in their bark and sap, to insects, fire, and decay. Everybody knew the trees were there, but they were considered unmarketable. There was no point in spending hundreds of thousands of dollars to build a road just to fetch several dozen cedar trees. Simpler to let them slowly rot.

We would never have schemed to steal even a single living tree, but the status of this cedar was ambiguous. A green, upright tree was private property, but in a few circumstances dead and down timber could belong to whoever had the ambition to remove it. This wasn't just a handy sophism. "Dead and down" was a category common in the timber industry; the phrase sometimes appeared even in sales contracts. Naturally there were differences of opinion as to when a tree was dead or even when it was down, and such decisions made cutting firewood a little more interesting. Did the tree have to be flat on the ground or could it just be leaning severely? Was it permissible to fell a snag that still had a couple of tufts of green needles, or did you have to wait till next year to drop it?

"Dead and down" is perhaps misleading, however, implying that once it was on the ground a tree was *hors de combat*, fit only for worms. But downed timber rotted slowly in the relatively dry Idaho climate, and a tree that was valueless for commercial lumber could make usable firewood even after a decade on the ground. And downed cedar was unique. These big trees rotted from the inside out, leaving a thick ring of dense, straight-grained wood that was prized locally as a source of roofing shingles, or shakes. A roof made of split cedar shakes was handsome, durable, and — if purchased from a building supply outlet — expensive. Looked at objectively, it might be said that the removal for conversion to personal use of enough cedar to shake even a fraction of the roofs in Coeur d'Alene would have been a flagrant act of grand larceny.

But there were mitigating circumstances. Let me try to explain why sometimes the line between scrounging and theft was hard to draw. The land in and around Alder Creek was owned by many different entities. Large-scale highway maps show much of the area lying within the borders of the St. Joe National Forest, but smaller survey maps show an amazing patchwork of private and public holdings. A relatively small amount of land, some ninety thousand acres, was under federal control. On all sides of the national forest lay the Coeur d'Alene tribe's tracts; the reservation operated more or less independently of state and federal agencies. Mingled with the national forest and tribal lands were many thousands of acres belonging to corporations based in Lewiston, Boise, or Seattle. Some of the timberland was actually owned by timber companies, but much of it belonged to the railroads, to Burlington Northern and to the Chicago, Milwaukee, and St. Paul.

For years, and for a variety of reasons, most of this land was little changed since the 1930s. Alder Creek had small appeal to real estate developers; its topography was unspectacular, and it was too far from a population center to market as recreational homesites. The climate was too cold and the terrain too steep for commercial agriculture; the land couldn't be drained, farmed, or settled on. To make money on it required an owner to take the long view, slowly and passively accumulating capital by growing trees. The land was of immediate interest only to the occasional hunter or to its owners at tax time.

Surrounded by these vast landholdings, and permitted for the most part to wander through them freely as we scrounged for mushrooms, firewood, or grouse, my neighbors and I lived like peasants on the manor, scratching out our lives by the grace and benevolence of our lords. Our obligations to Pacific Crown, Diamond International, and Potlatch were fewer and less onerous than medieval peasants' duties to their masters — we simply had to close gates and keep roads clear of debris and use care in camping and hunting. In return, we understood we had the "right" to collect for personal use a reasonable amount of dead and down timber. The timber corporations can be accused of many things, but it is surely to their credit that they acknowledged, if only tacitly, their obligations to the handful of people who dwelt within their domains. In this case at least, trickle-down economics worked to perfection, the needs of the poor being amply satisfied by the leavings of the rich.

That splendid anachronism thrills me even now. In 1974, in the United States of America, a very small number of people lived according to a principle first enunciated in the Anglo-Saxon codes of medieval England: to the peasants belonged the windfalls. And in the summer of that year, cedar that had lain untouched for longer than I had been alive seemed to Jacobsen and me to belong in the category of windfall.

This custom was preserved only because there was no real market for dead and down timber. In retrospect, I can see a direct connection between the worthlessness of dead and down wood and the richness of life in Alder Creek.

All that changed suddenly in 1975 when the country ran short of oil. The energy crisis of the mid- and late seventies made wood heat hugely popular, and soon it also made lawbreakers out of us.

Evidence for this reclassification of dead wood from waste to commodity spread through Alder Creek like a metabolic disorder. Up until the oil embargo, wood heat had been waning in popularity for decades. Now, almost overnight, my neighbors with their fussy wood stoves were no longer considered crazy eccentrics or riffraff. We woke up one morning, feet and fingers freezing because the fire had gone out, and discovered to our surprise that we were the avant-garde of the housing industry. Revolution was in the air. Oil was extinct; wood heat was the wave of the future. Magazines and newspapers in their Sunday supplements published articles on the care and feeding of wood stoves; old stoves rusting in barns were cleaned out, polished up, and pressed into service; new stoves began to appear on the market, at first slowly, the products of cottage industry, then in great numbers. For a short time the Ashley stove (as advertised in Stewart Brand's bible of the counterculture, *The Whole Earth Catalog*) set the standard. Then, in a triumph of slick marketing, Ashley was surpassed by the Scandinavian Jøtul. And soon Jøtul was just one stove among many, competing with a half-dozen other brands for floor space and ad copy.

From one point of view it was an amazing success story. The need for firewood brought with it some greater measures of prosperity. New businesses developed to serve the wood-heat phenomenon. St. Maries opened one new chain-saw shop, then a second; chimney sweeps advertised in the Spokane papers; hardware stores moved stovepipe, dampers, and soot brushes from the back room to the main sales area. And suddenly the firewood business became big business. Now the woods on weekends were full of a new kind of woodcutter. We saw flatbeds, we saw semitrailers. They came in teams, a couple of small trucks escorting a big one. The license plates identified them as coming from the north, typically the counties around Coeur d'Alene or Spokane, and they rolled past our place loaded down with alarming amounts of wood. I have no right to condemn them; they were only practicing on a large scale what I did on one much smaller. The only difference was that everybody knew that woodcutting like that didn't have much of a future.

The end, when it came, came quickly. One year good firewood trees were plentiful and easily obtained. Three years later, you might drive along logging roads and firebreaks for several miles and not spot a single dead tamarack or red fir accessible by road or skid trail. They are all gone. Now in the summers we burn the so-called trash woods with little heat value, usually white fir gone partly to punk, and many year-round residents of Alder Creek warm their homes with pellet stoves or with propane. Increasingly now, if you drive down roads newly cut through the timber, the way is blocked by tubular steel gates or dirt bars heaped across the road by Caterpillar tractors. More and more, the timber corporations, having logged a section of land, will conclude by denying the public access to it. Or they will draw up a secondary logging contract that conveys to a single buyer the "rights" to any leftover trash or deadwood. Or they will, as I have sometimes seen, simply bulldoze the dead and down trees into a huge slash pile and burn them. A way of life that persisted for more than three quarters of a century vanished in a few short seasons.

Who should take the blame? Many would say it's the same combination of stupidity and greed that settled the West in the first place. That's how the West was lost, they say. The West's history is boom-and-bust: people swarmed to wherever the gold or beavers or trees were, and when those commodities ran out, they left ruins behind. For me, though, finding somebody or some innate American quality to blame is too simplistic. Ten thousand miles away from the Idaho panhandle, the disruption in the Middle Eastern oil supply began a process that ultimately affected the rhythms of life in Alder Creek.

I don't see any clear lesson in this sad tangle of opportunity, temptation, shortsightedness, and bad luck. And it's hard to identify a villain worthy of the name, unless it's the concept of a market economy; the firewood business became big business mainly because there were no available options to the insistent presence of money. That putting a price on a thing is a uniquely sinister way of destroying it is scarcely a novel insight, but living well in Alder Creek was partly the art of bending the constraints of property and ownership. Once firewood trees became commodities to be bought and sold like wheat or pork bellies, they became trapped in the mechanics of trade. I am reminded of the conclusion that Thoreau drew from his experiences on Walden Pond. "Trade," he wrote, "curses everything it handles; and though you trade in messages from heaven, the whole curse of trade attaches to the business."

10

Backwoods Mechanics

EINO JACOBSEN decided in 1976 to run for election to the board of the Benewah Valley Association. He announced his candidacy bluntly at the annual nominating meeting. "You all know me," he said. "I'm the guy whose rig has broke down in front of the mailboxes of everybody who's sitting in this room."

Jacobsen didn't win the election, but his words made sense as an electoral platform for several reasons. Accustomed to dealing with their own ailing cars, people in Alder Creek listened with relish to tales of others' breakdowns. Fixing broken vehicles was one of the chief ways my friends and I made time to get together and talk. Men and women alike had to learn a good deal about what made rigs run, and, more important, what made them stop running. Halfway through my third winter in Alder Creek I wrote out a list of the parts I'd had to learn how to replace to keep my car running. It made an impressive résumé: new piston rings, new intake and exhaust valves, oil seals for the rear main bearing and the front and rear differentials, a speedometer worm drive, a transfer gear, an exhaust manifold, two sets of U-joints and two pairs of ball joints for the drive shafts and steering linkage, respectively, a generator and a voltage regulator (these lifted from an old Chevrolet and pressed into emergency service), and a rear main leaf spring. And still, like most of my neighbors, I was driving a car that likely as not would strand me at unforseen moments in awkward places.

Actually, our cars almost never completely stranded us. They just ran worse and worse and took up more and more of the day with thinking how to circumvent their quirks. Cotton Stanridge, the patriarch of one of the first families of Alder Creek, ran his truck for years without brakes. "I take it real slow" was how he explained it to me. It was the same with Jacobsen; his 1949 International was plagued with mysterious faults in the wiring harness, and it could be seen almost daily, abandoned somewhere by the roadside. After it had spent an hour or two in repose, it started right up. Bill Fletcher's panel van had no reverse gear; he always made sure to park no closer than twenty feet from the nearest obstacle in front of him so he had room to turn around by driving forward.

We accommodated our cars' shortcomings the way we might have adjusted to the eccentricities of a friend. Running with oil or coolant leaks was common. So were bad tires; for months I drove with a tire that leaked fifteen pounds of air each week, no more, no less. When the rear axle broke, I engaged the front hubs. To compensate for a malfunctioning generator, I had to leave the house half an hour early each day to be sure to arrive at the university in time to park in one particular spot near the top of a long hill. That way I could coast down the hill to jump-start the car, conserving precious electrical capacity in the battery.

Living in a rural landscape, I saw with great clarity how fully the car expresses our nation's character and dreams. We were utterly dependent on our cars. On them we counted for life and liberty; with them we pursued happiness. Even the local newspaper seemed determined to subordinate life to travel by car. The *St. Maries Gazette Record* devoted about six inches of column space each week to so-called news from the various regions around town, news collected by correspondents from Fernwood or the Benewah Valley or "Upriver." It was the residents' comings and goings that always seemed to the editors to be newsworthy; the main thing was to have gone someplace by car. Readers discovered that "Linda Tunick of Pullman drove to Bill and Nancy Gruber's house on Alder Creek last week" or that "Tom and Dottie Hodgson drove to Moses Lake on Tuesday to inspect their ranch." It was an amusing caricature of Robert Louis Stevenson's notion that to travel hopefully is better than to arrive. The most extreme case told how a woman was driven by her husband to the Benewah Community Hospital in St. Maries, where, the story added, almost as an afterthought, she had died.

The high and low points of my backwoods mechanicking came together in September of 1976. That year I was driving a rebuilt 1955 Willys station wagon. I had bought it the previous winter from Fred Rainbolt. Rainbolt had a reputation as the finest mechanic in the area. It was well deserved. He also had a reputation for stinginess, also accurate. I had never met anyone who so closely estimated the margin between personal investment and return. He showed me the summer kitchen he had built for his wife, Nina. "The studs was all culls from the mill at Post Falls," Rainbolt said, beaming. "I only had two left over when I was done." Another time he took me fishing. We went for catfish, which he said was the only kind of fish he could catch in sufficient numbers to justify his time and effort. We gathered worms from one of Nina's flower beds. Fred stuck two welding rods into the ground, then taped one of the bared ends of an electrical cord to each rod and plugged it in. The worms came pouring out of the soft earth, desperately seeking relief from the surge of current. Within minutes we collected more than a hundred worms.

Rainbolt lived in relative isolation from many of his neighbors, and he often spoke disparagingly of them. I was never really sure why they didn't get along. I'd heard that Fred had alienated people by taking over the school bus route. Rumor had it that he had somehow discovered the lowest bid, which was made by the local family who'd held the bus contract for years, and then underbid that by a dollar. Another story hinted at a feud involving Fred's well. It was drilled at community expense, in exchange for water rights for the one-room schoolhouse that sat on the edge of Rainbolt's property, rights that Fred supposedly never acknowledged. Fred naturally saw it differently; he complained that the school kids always left the tap open and drained his reservoir. Mainly it was Fred's thriftiness that people remembered. I mentioned his name once to Dick Benge, who knew Fred from some years back when they both worked for Potlatch. Benge, the sweetest man I'd ever met, asked simply, "Is Fred still squeezing his nickels till they holler?"

But Fred was always fair with me. He knew we had no money, and so he sold us the Willys for $1,000 — $300 down. Fred said he'd take the rest in firewood I could give him over the next couple of years. The deal was pretty ragged, structured as it was on firewood futures, not to mention the future of firewood in general. But I had no alternative. I wrote Fred a check and he gave me the keys.

The Willys station wagon was a remarkable machine, the no-nonsense prototype of latter-day sport-utility vehicles. I liked its mechanical simplicity, especially after years of fighting the eccentricities of a worn-out Land Rover. I also liked its outdated, hugely chromed style and the flamboyant accessories with which Rainbolt had equipped it. Mounted on the front bumper was an eight-thousand-pound winch that took power off the engine. The Willys came with freewheeling hubs on the front axle and two five-gallon gas cans, one mounted on each side at the front where the fenders — they were real fenders, broad arches of steel that curved gracefully up and over the front wheels — narrowed to meet the passenger compartment. Inside the car were gauges for oil pressure, water temperature, electrical output, and engine manifold vacuum. There was a hand throttle to govern the speed of the winch when it was engaged, and there were fold-down jump seats in the rear.

Of course it came with a gun rack — all trucks in Alder Creek came with gun racks. But the Willys had two. The first was the conventional kind that you see on the rear windows of pickups, often carrying fishing rods, map cases, or umbrellas. That one was mounted on the side immediately behind the driver's seat. The second gun rack had been handcrafted by Rainbolt and mounted on the floor, just inside the door by the driver's left foot.

"I never did like reaching around behind my head for a loaded gun," he said and grinned, pride extending his smile up to touch his high cheekbones. "Now I don't even have to get out of the car to shoot a grouse."

Rainbolt's homemade gun rack was a marvel of inspiration. In this it was typical of the ingenious devices I often saw in homes and vehicles in rural Idaho. It consisted of two pieces, a small cookie cutter–shaped socket welded to the floor and a felt-lined clamp bolted to the dashboard just left of the steering wheel. The butt of the gun rested on the floor in the socket, and the forepiece clamped firmly to the dash. It reminded me of the gun mounts I'd seen on stagecoaches in old western movies, positioned right at the feet of the guard so he could grab his weapon quickly to fend off bandits.

I was absurdly fond of that gun rack. Napoleon discovered that soldiers would follow him anywhere just for the pleasure of receiving a bit of colored ribbon; that was how I felt about my gun rack. I was convinced that I had struck the deal of the decade, and for the next several months I happily set off to work each morning in a car with two gun racks but no hand brake, horn, or working heater.

Or an oil filter. The Willys did not have an oil filter. I asked Rainbolt about that, and he said that the engine he had installed as a replacement in the Willys, a rebuilt Plymouth flathead, had never had an external oil filter. That was a modern addition to engine design, Rainbolt said. The way he put it made oil filters sound vaguely suspect, like iodine in salt or fluoridated water.

"Plymouth didn't ever put oil filters in them engines," he said. "Change the oil regularly," he added, "and it'll be fine."

I did, and it wasn't. To be fair, something entirely different may have killed the car. But after I had run it through the winter of 1975 and into the next spring, the engine began to consume oil. Lots of oil. It soon became impossible to nurse it. It spewed out huge clouds of blue smoke that were illegal long before emissions tests became federally mandated. It smoked so much that even in Idaho, where the highway patrols were predisposed to cut wheezing rigs some slack, I once got a ticket. "I'm going to have to write you a citation for defective equipment," the cop said, almost apologetically. It was a moment to savor, pure northern Idaho, to be sitting by the roadside trying to assure the person in uniform writing you a ticket that he was doing the right thing. I told him I agreed one hundred percent with his assessment: "It's a real piece of shit," I said.

The problem wasn't only money. I was a victim of the infamous obsolescence American manufacturers planned for their products. No one closer than Seattle stocked replacement parts for a twenty-year-old engine. To order a new piston meant a delay of a week to ten days — in 1976, the concept of next-day shipping for automotive parts was unknown. I had torn the engine down Saturday morning; the car had to be drivable by Sunday night. Somewhere in Alder Creek there had to be a piston to fit my engine. I called Rainbolt, then Mullan, than Strobel, all without luck, and then I remembered that Bill McPherson had a 1953 Plymouth sedan parked in the back of his yard. So I called him to see if the car still had an engine in it.

McPherson came to pick me up, and together we drove back to his house to look at the car. I should say that McPherson was concerned about my troubles, and he truly wished to help me. He was among my best friends, and in the past he had often come to my aid with tools or goods. We first rummaged around his shop until we found one of the little bottles of grain alcohol he had stashed in about a half-dozen places. His breathing rattled happily as he fussed with the cap: "Heh heh heh, heh heh heh, heh heh heh." McPherson purposely hid the bottles of booze around his shop, knowing that he'd forget where they were; that way, while working, he'd occasionally uncover one and have an excuse for a small celebration. We each took a drink, and then we got down to serious negotiations. "What would you take for one of the pistons off that engine?" I asked.

McPherson weighed my request courteously but skeptically.

Had I tried Brown's Salvage in Spokane?

Didn't Billy Fletcher have a Plymouth sitting by his woodshed?

What about Fleet Parts in St. Maries?

"Anyways," he said, "I think them pistons was oversized twenty thousandths."

By that time I had learned enough about cars to tell good advice from bad, and McPherson's doubts sounded like rationalizations. It seemed crazy that a man would not want to give up a piston from an engine in a car that but for the slow pull of gravity had sat immobile in a corner of his yard since Lyndon Johnson was in the White House. Weeds grew high around the engine and in the trunk, and vermin wintered in the passenger compartment. The seats and interior trim were ruinous; what cloth, rubber, and plastic had escaped the mice's gnawings, the suns of more than twenty summers had bleached to gossamer fragility. It all crumbled at a touch. The car would never run again. Yet McPherson seemed reluctant to surrender a piston, and the more we talked, the more I had the impression that he was trying to make his way through an ethical problem.

The choice was not simply between cheapness and generosity, although that was part of it. McPherson lived up to his Scots stereotype in many ways. He was famous locally for waiting more than a decade to install indoor plumbing until he had assembled, by barter or by scrounging, all the parts he needed free of charge. But the car's hold on McPherson was more ambiguous. It was as if he believed that someday the car would run. Against that vision he weighed the needs of a friend.

Like many of the people I came to know in the West, McPherson was foolishly optimistic. Despite his age and relative poverty, his chronic and severe coronary ailments, belief in a better tomorrow seemed bred in him as surely as his pale highlander's eyes or his tendency to baldness. Years ago, that car had been positioned at that spot in the yard with a purpose, however unspoken, with a dream, however unformed. To begin now to part the car out was in some ways, therefore, an admission of his own failure. Better it should slowly waste away, rusting to dust in unviolated desolation, than to be torn apart. To remove a piston from that car was a desecration, visible proof of a fallen world.

This was a pattern of response I saw time and again among my neighbors. They were generous with their time and emotion beyond all expectation and often contrary to all personal gain, but they clung to material goods with comical ferocity. Ed Strobel parked two cars, a travel trailer, and, in an incredible burst of faith, a Studebaker truck on his property when he and Jean moved

to Alder Creek in the summer of 1971. Several times I asked Stro-
bel if he wanted to sell the trailer, but he answered only in vague
terms. And once, on a day when I was near panicked that parts for
British cars were unobtainable in northern Idaho, I asked Strobel
if I could buy the Studebaker engine to install in the Land Rover.
The potential result of that transplant would have been auto-
motive madness — an engine from a vehicle whose manufacturer
no longer existed, powering a car no longer imported. Strobel
hemmed and hawed. "I was thinking," he said, "I might get the
truck running this summer." Nearly twenty years later, cars, truck,
and trailer were abandoned exactly as parked when, Jean dead,
Strobel left Idaho for good. As far as I know, they rest there yet.

In the end, McPherson let me tear down his engine and remove
a piston. Still, I know he regretted it. Many times afterward when
I saw him, he teased me that I had wasted a perfectly good engine.
Even years later, after we had moved away from Alder Creek and
had become merely summer folks, McPherson seemed unable to
let go of the memory of what he considered my greatest folly.
There was never any bitterness or reproach in him, only wry
humor. To an outsider, McPherson would have seemed absurdly
Scotch. What difference could it make whether an engine lay in
the grass with six pistons or five? But McPherson took a longer
view: one day, in a better world, his engine would run.

The actual installation of the piston was an exercise in despera-
tion. Just as McPherson had recollected, the piston was oversized.
Not by much, but when you are trying to make parts fit inside an
engine, a mismatch of twenty thousandths of an inch is a huge
obstacle. It was Sunday afternoon, the sun was lowering in the
sky, and I had to be at work fifty-seven miles away the follow-
ing morning. What to do? I did the only thing I could think of
to make the piston fit. I got out my orbital sander and started to
grind it down.

I reasoned that if I could keep the piston nearly round, the new
rings would hold compression for a while. Whether "a while"
would be ten miles or a thousand I had no way of knowing. It

took several hours of error and trial, but in the end I was able to insert the piston into the bore. Then I bolted the head and crankcase pan back on and hoped for the best.

In fact the fit was better than one might have expected. The ground-down piston functioned well the next day on the drive to and from work. Oil consumption was eliminated, and the engine ran strongly until one day nearly a month later when, chugging up the last of the three long grades on Highway 95 before entering Moscow, the engine threw a connecting rod. The many months of running starved for oil had weakened the bearings, and one of them finally shattered. The rod made a horrible noise as it slammed up and down on the spinning crankshaft, and as I limped the last few miles into town I had much leisure to try out different metaphors to describe the sound. Hammers in a washing machine seemed best. I parked the Willys in a university lot, where it gathered dust and tickets until weeks later, when I towed it home. The Willys sat in the front yard until the next summer, when I bartered an old parlor stove for a used but running Plymouth engine, pulled from a car that had cracked its transmission housing on a rock in the Benewah Road. After I installed the new engine, I traded the Willys, in a neat twist of circumstances, to McPherson. What Victorian farce could be more tightly plotted? In exchange for the Willys I received a fifteen-foot boat with an outboard motor. McPherson, in turn, gave the Willys to his son, the deputy sheriff in St. Maries. Now and then I saw the car in or about town, apparently still roadworthy.

Months later, out of curiosity, I pulled the head and oil pan from the broken engine in order to inspect my makeshift piston. I discovered that the breakdown had occurred in another cylinder; *my* piston and rod looked just fine. It pleased me to know that at the time the engine died, the homemade piston was functioning capably. And who knows? Maybe it would have run like that for years.

11

Why They Shoot Bears
in Alder Creek

FOR MY DAUGHTERS as for Nancy and me, books were central parts of our lives. Many of the children's books we bought were about animals: from Beatrix Potter's various rodent narratives to Disney's entertainment industry, these animals of the mind provided endless amusement and wonder. The book I was reading to my daughters, Elaine and Laura, one morning belonged to a series of books we'd bought by Stan and Jan Berenstain, all of them about bears; this one was *Bears on Wheels*. The language was rhythmic and incantatory; both girls loved it. I had just got to the part where two troupes of bears were hurtling toward each other on their unicycles when I was interrupted by someone knocking at the door. It was Duke Martin. He seemed formal and diffident — as always, he seemed perpetually embarrassed to be standing in someone else's house — but eventually he got to the point: could I give him a hand dressing a bear he had just shot down by the creek? Pulling on my boots and coat, I puzzled over this quirky conjuration. If it shed no light on the relationship between art and life, it was proof at least that in Alder Creek, bears were always on our minds.

It's impossible to live for very long in rural north Idaho without coming into contact with large wild animals, especially bears. Our bears are the sort called black bears, and, as most any guidebook or encyclopedia will tell you, black bears can be any color from white to cinnamon to sienna. Sometimes they are even black. Like most wild animals, black bears avoid humans whenever possible. The trouble is that there are so many bears in Idaho's backcountry that avoiding humans is not always possible. What's worse, for all their shyness or even fear of humans, black bears also know that they are big and powerful animals that can pursue their activities with an unvarying fixity of purpose. Thus the black bear's alleged shyness coexists with what can only be called arrogance, and with that arrogance comes a fair measure of unpredictability. Everybody I knew in Idaho who worked even occasionally in the woods had at least one bear story. This is mine.

In July and August of 1976 I spent more time than ever in the woods, cutting firewood to work off the debt I owed Rainbolt for his Willys station wagon. By midsummer I had cut maybe twenty-five cords, and I felt I had everything under control. One day Greg Mullan, at age fourteen the oldest of Mullan's children, came along to help me. The tree I had found was ideally placed. It stood about fifty yards off the road on the uphill side. It was a big tamarack snag, straight and well away from any other trees that could impede its falling. It was nearly tall enough to reach the road when it fell, and the slope of the land was steep enough and free of brush so that many of the rounds, once I cut them free, would roll down to the road.

The felling and the bucking were uneventful, a labor of habit. The wood was among the best I'd ever cut — dry, deep yellow-orange and straight-grained — and the tree was one of the few I had felled big enough to make two truckloads. It was at least thirty inches across at the butt end, and from time to time as I sawed my way up the trunk I was surprised by the way the rounds looked foreshortened. I was sawing sixteen-inch lengths for the parlor stove, and against the large diameter that length looked wrong. Rolling and bouncing down the hillside, the rounds looked thin and comical.

The work went swiftly; within an hour I had sawed enough for the first load. Four or five of the bigger rounds picked up enough momentum to bump across the road and into some chest-high brush on the downhill side. I didn't want to lose what was possibly three days' warmth, so I told Greg I'd retrieve the runaway rounds. I made several forays into the brush to find them, and I rolled them back uphill, annoyed at having to move my wood twice. I shoved them out of the brush onto the road. Then I sat down on the bumper of the truck to catch my breath. Greg sat on the bumper too, in the way that youths sometimes flatter adults by unthinkingly taking on their gestures. As we sat there, not more than ten yards in front of us we saw the bear shuffle onto the road.

Seeing is very much a matter of expectation; unless you know what you're looking for, you don't know what you're looking at. Big predators especially appear so seldom and so unexpectedly that you often see them as something else. I have seen bears I took to be large dogs or cattle, and once, as I watched a mountain lion move across a meadow toward the timber, I saw at first only a house cat stalking through the grass. Yet at the same time I remember marveling at how a cat was clearly visible at a distance of some two hundred yards.

So it was with this bear. In the mid-seventies stockmen could still turn their cattle loose just about anywhere, and it was not uncommon to come across stray cattle in the woods. So when I saw a large black animal stumble out of the brush I wondered what had caused a medium-sized Angus steer to be this far upcountry. Not until the animal had moved entirely onto the road and paused to stare at Greg and me did I see a bear.

The bear stood in the middle of the road, solemn and rigid, and stared at us. The time we spent gazing at each other can't have been more than a few seconds, but it seemed much longer. The animal had emerged from the brush at the same place I had stood to shove the stray firewood onto the road. It spooked me to think that only moments before we had shared the same patch of brush.

The bear took a few steps toward the opposite side of the road, and as he moved I went cautiously to the cab of the truck to fetch the shotgun lying on the seat. If the bear attacked, the gun would be all but useless — the shells were number eight birdshot. But I had seen too many movies not to act out a part I thought I had to play. It was odd to feel frightened and foolish at the same time.

All of the six or eight other bears I had seen in four Idaho summers I saw only in retreat from humans. In the normal relations between man and bear, so I had heard, the animal would flee. But rarely, and for reasons nobody really understood, a bear would attack. I'd read that both behaviors were motivated by fear. A bear shunned encounters with humans unless there was some good reason not to — when protecting cubs, for example, or when the animal felt cornered.

This bear was different. It did not seem openly hostile, but it was not afraid of us either. I wondered whether it could close the distance between us before Greg and I could hide in the cab of the truck. It was clearly a face-off, and in such a situation there's not much you can do. Two alien species gaze at each other, as John Berger puts it in *About Looking*, "across an abyss of non-comprehension." The bear had that particular kind of self-conscious style that in a human we might call confidence. It was unnerving to confront a wild animal powerful enough to regard you with something like scorn. Meanwhile, the bear stravaged about the roadside and the fringe of the uphill slope. It may have been thinking, "I see no need to alter my plans simply because a man and a boy happen to be nearby." Or, worse, it may have been contemplating the bear equivalent of "Go ahead, make my day."

When the bear had strayed about ten yards up the road I fired the gun in the air. I hoped the noise would startle the animal into flight, but of course the only reason I had for thinking that was that I had seen it done in films. I knew right away it was a dumb idea. The shot startled me all right — a twelve-gauge shotgun makes a hell of a blast with only the wind sighing in the trees for competition — but the bear only stopped and stared. I would have sworn it was reading my mind. Its behavior was entirely leisurely, almost rational. It slowly traversed the uphill slope, moving two or three steps, browsing in the duff, stopping, turning to regard us, then moving again. After a long while it vanished near the top of the slope, several hundred feet away.

Except for the moments when I was unwittingly alone with the bear in the brush I guess there had never been any real danger, and yet by the time the bear disappeared both Greg and I were exhausted. Greg asked what I wanted to do. By then I was calm enough to view the whole thing with irony.

"You load the truck, son," I said, trying to sound like John Wayne in *The Cowboys.* "I'll watch for bears."

I looked at Greg to see what he thought of my attempt at humor, but he was too young and still too excited to let go of the gravity of the event, and he assumed I was just giving him an order. He nodded and turned to walk to the wood. Later that morning, after both of us had loaded the truck and were halfway down the mountain, we met Nancy and my daughters coming toward us in the Willys. They were worried because of our tardiness and had come to help. It was a great occasion, now in the company of an escort, to be driving home with a fine load of wood and the tale of an adventure.

I like to tell the bear story. I return sometimes to the place where it happened, even though each year it becomes more difficult to find. Erosion and new growth quickly transform beyond recognition one small spot in the woods. But the place never loses its hold on me. I have pictures of myself holding my son, then two years old, pointing out to him the precise line of shrubs through which the bear had emerged fourteen years before. In the way of small children he likes to hear the story of the bear told over and over. I guess he believes it's one of the few moments of real excitement his father has ever had, and he has a ritual of questions that he wants me to answer every time I tell it. "Where exactly," he asks, "was the bear?" "Didn't you even hear it?" "Why didn't the bear run away when it saw the gun?" And, "Why did you tell Greg to load the truck?"

I have to conclude that for my son, as I think for me, the tale of the bear defines an archetypal experience between large, fierce animals and humans that is almost lost. I think that day in the woods we came to a mutual acknowledgment, man and bear, an accord a little like the fabulous bargains between humans and wild animals that are described in myths. I am reluctant to go so far as to say that to really get to know a bear you have to be willing to shoot it, but at some level my encounter on that day tells me that this is so, that the lives of animals and humans are linked historically by violence. Neither zoos nor, I have come to believe, encounters with such animals in wilderness preserves duplicate this experience.

Take the case of the grizzly. Once this great bear, the most formidable predator in the Western Hemisphere, ranged widely throughout North America. When the *Mayflower* lay anchored off the coast of what would become Massachusetts and when *King Lear* debuted at the Globe, it is thought that there roamed in the regions west of the Mississippi River as many as fifty thousand of the bears identified ominously but appropriately as *Ursus horribilis*.

Fifty thousand bears. Not bears of every kind and description, but, in addition to the tens of thousands of other sorts of bears, fifty thousand grizzly bears. When I first came across that information I was curious. I imagined all those bears dispersed across the western countryside like a football team in a zone defense. I fetched a calculator and distributed the bears over the land area of the western states just to get some idea of their average population density.

With this arithmetic I hoped to glimpse more clearly what life must have been like in Alder Creek early in the twentieth century. It was only a crude estimate, and I claim nothing substantial for it. Of course there had been no grizzlies at all in the thousands of square miles of western deserts, and so the bears' population densities would have been somewhat higher once the large uninhabitable regions were factored out. Still, the numbers were educative. It worked out to about one grizzly bear for every thirty-five or forty square miles, or roughly one bear for every piece of country six miles square.

That sounds like a pretty low density, and so it is; the early settlers in Alder Creek would not have been tripping over grizzlies as they went outside to their privies each morning. The country was big enough so that humans and grizzlies could go about their respective business. But not so big — here is the sobering point — the country was not so big that the bear would ever disappear from your consciousness. When you're used to roaming the land-scape freely, as we did when we lived in Alder Creek, it's easy to make your presence felt over an area six miles on a side. Eventu-ally there's not a hillside you don't explore, not a valley you don't consider somehow your own. The same holds true for the bear. One grizzly for each six-mile square. For the people homesteading within that range, therefore, the bear is always out there some-where, always at the limits of consciousness. You probably don't think about it much at all, but it's there all the same, a savage and random potential that you can never entirely ignore.

All this is thrilling or frightening, depending on your point of view. In the early 1900s, if you lived in Alder Creek long enough, you would meet the bear. It was a simple matter of probability and statistics that reflects the constant comings and goings of you and the bear. One day your paths would converge, and what would happen was anybody's guess. I pictured myself living at that time, in that place, with those conditions. I imagined the bear's and my own separate movements, seemingly random and yet, like the *Titanic* and the iceberg, perfectly coordinated. The bear repre-sented the world's mysterious hostility to my own human pres-ence, a hostility that, without the example of the dangerous ani-mal, might well have been inexpressible.

I marvel at my ancestors' courage in living daily with that dread, just as some future minds will doubtless marvel at the non-chalance with which people today bore the risks of negotiating a car at high speed in heavy traffic. Or, sad to say, the courage with which children attend school, knowing that one of their class-mates may well be armed and dangerous. In the end, in all these cases, you trust less to your skill than to luck and to God. Of course you could always choose not to play the game, or to change the rules. You could hunt the bear, force a deadly encounter, and end the game entirely. And who knows? Had I lived in Alder Creek in 1895 or 1910 I might have done just that.

My own encounter with the bear seemed to be in this way ele-mental. We were autonomous parties in a chance encounter, equally free to decide whether to attack or withdraw. Without my option to meet the bear's attack (whether an attack was a real possibility or simply imagined makes no difference), the episode would lack its defining *frisson*. The basis of the encounter was my acknowledgment that I would kill the bear (or somehow try to, with birdshot), because not to do so would have been to disavow the sense of obligation I suddenly felt to a fourteen-year-old boy and his family.

This obligation, I suspect, in some obscure way lay behind some of my neighbors' obsessions with ridding the woods of bears. The bear was not an abstract concept or a symbol of a vanished wilderness. To them, and, as I discovered, to me also, it was clear evidence of the hostile reciprocity of nature; the bear stood for "the first circle," as John Berger says, "of what surrounded man."

To many readers, this kind of attitude will seem ignorant, belligerent, and primitive. A common assumption of much recent writing on nature is that what I'm saying is just more of the same kind of macho thinking that got us and hundreds of endangered species in trouble in the first place. Benevolence and enlightened tolerance of the animals' wildness, so the argument runs, are the appropriate attitudes to adopt in our relations with animals.

I don't dispute most of this. If we're to conserve the world's animal populations, doubtless we must cease slaughtering them. But without potentially lethal interactions of the sort I've described, fierce animals like bears are going to be as peripheral to human imagination as if they were all shut away in zoos.

That's the irony that we face in coming to terms with large predatory animals. Central to our ancient relationship with them were their dangerousness and our legitimate response to it. These seem destined to be superseded by an artificial sense of stewardship that is probably necessary but in some ways bankrupt. It *is* often this simple: us or them. I admire the sentiments of Rick Bass when he writes, in *The Lost Grizzlies,* of the efforts to find suitable refuge for the few hundred bears that remain in the contiguous United States. To shunt them off to designated preserves is the only way it seems possible to save them. What else can we do? But shunting the grizzlies to a few restricted territories amounts to a cultural and imaginative marginalization, and for me that choice is as un-satisfactory as it seems necessary. Wilderness, like nature, may well be a value concept; and if we define our encounters with bears in terms of the contrast their wildness provides with our civilized lives, we make those animals, in Berger's memorable phrase, "the starting point of a daydream: a point from which the day-dreamer departs with his back turned."

12

At the Bend in the River
Where the Cottonwoods Grow

I MET Frank Burger one afternoon in the summer of 1976. For several weeks I had been stockpiling the firewood I was going to use to pay off the Willys, and it was soon obvious that the pile of wood in the back yard was too big to be intended for just one household. So Burger stopped by the house to ask if any of the wood was for sale. I told him it wasn't, and then I told him what I was planning to do with it, and as we talked I mentioned the troubles I'd had that morning with a bear. He pulled from his pocket three twelve-gauge slugs and told me to use them instead of bird-shot the next time a bear bothered me. The slugs scared me a little; each one had the heft of a roll of pennies. We talked some more, and by the time he left I had agreed to deliver five or six truckloads of wood to the place he had just signed on to caretake.

The ranch on which Frank Burger lived lay in a meadow on a hill about a hundred yards from the St. Maries River. You first saw the ranch from a promontory high above it. So steep was the terrain that you saw no slope trailing away below you. Instead, you looked out as though from a battlement over the tops of trees growing on the downhill side of the road. Beyond the trees, the distance and difference in altitude giving it a more delicate tint, almost the wash of watercolors, was the ranch. In the four years we had lived in Alder Creek we had many times driven past that ranch, looking down on its log house from where the River Road ran along the promontory, three hundred feet above and a mile away, and we had always wondered who was privileged to live there. It was the house I would have chosen to live in over anywhere else in the world, and now on this afternoon the man who lived there stood before me and invited me to deliver his firewood. I felt as if I'd just won some cosmic lottery.

Burger was naturally gregarious, and unlike some of the other solitary old men I knew in Idaho, he often spoke of his past. He told us of his marriages, his family, and his jobs. The tales he told us over the years we knew him sometimes sounded preposterous. It seemed improbable that he had slept with Jane Russell or that he knew firsthand about big game hunting in Africa. All the same, Burger's conversation was straight and unaffected, and I never discovered in it a contradiction that would prove he spoke anything but truth.

I could only guess at his education. Born in Illinois, he had, so he said, run away from home at fourteen and never looked back. His speech had quirks and idiosyncrasies I'd never before encountered — he habitually said "evidently" when he meant "probably" — and he referred to the dark meat on fowl as "blue meat." As for his taste in reading, it was confined to the novels of Louis Lamour. Dozens of Lamour's novels lay scattered about his house. But I never saw him reading one, and every time he wrote a check to me to pay for firewood he asked me to fill it out. Burger simply affixed an indecipherable scrawl to the completed document.

More than once I saw him live up to some of his stories. When the ranch's owners decided they wanted the big log house for their own use, Burger built a new house largely on his own. He hauled rock from the riverbed for the footings, laid the concrete blocks for the basement walls and chimney, and teetered dangerously on a set of wooden planks while he nailed down the trusses for the roof. And he was a crack shot. On his way to cut firewood a grouse crossed the road in front of his truck and scrambled into the brush, where it huddled motionless next to a fallen log. Burger stopped the truck and took his .22 rifle out from behind the seat. "Where is it?" he said. I tried to describe its location, but to Burger's eyes the bird was perfectly camouflaged. "How far is it from the branch? Is he standing or sitting?" After hearing my crude coordinates, based on where he thought the bird was, Burger made the shot.

He was in all respects well suited to care for a large estate. Despite his poverty — he lived on social security and a small "railroad pension," as he put it — he treated his guests well. Burger made it his business to learn what they liked to eat or drink, and if on your first visit he lacked your favorite drink or snack, you could be sure he would have it when you returned. He bought bourbon and beer for Nancy and me, and he kept on hand a half-dozen varieties of penny candy for Elaine and Laura — licorice, gummi bears, peppermints, and an assortment of chocolates.

Burger was a born host, jovial and generous; more than once he told me to regard everything in his house as mine. He was a handsome man, even for his age. He was only of average height, but his bearing was striking, and you had the feeling that if he chose to he could impose his will by sheer force of presence. By medical standards his health was fair at best. He suffered increasingly from emphysema and often had to stop what he was doing, as he put it, "to catch my breathe." Yet in looking at him you saw only strength. You knew that here was someone with courage and who loved danger. More than once I saw men half his age kowtow before him like little boys, and women were smitten with him. Old and young women alike flirted with him; they felt safe and free in his presence. My daughters, then aged one and four, crawled all over him. Nancy's grandmother, well into her eighties, fell for him and joked about marriage. And Jean Strobel, a witty and cynical woman, forgot her cares and ailments and got drunk one night at a party at Burger's house and spent much of the evening lustily singing "I Drink My Whiskey from an Old Tin Cup." The only people he seemed not to like were timid souls; anybody who seemed to be in that category he dismissed as a "crying Jesus."

Old age only added to Burger's male authority, so that he seemed to have assumed, certainly in part by conscious choice, the image of a patriarch. His flowing white beard was an emblem of both geniality and masculine power. When you visited him you

had the sense that you had dropped in on a medieval king. Or on
Santa Claus.

It was a strange and heady experience to come and go in a land-
scape that resembled a movie set. Burger's ranch was visible only
from a distance. Framed from a single vantage point, your view of
it seemed calculated for aesthetic effect, in the style of Japanese
gardens. Coming upriver from St. Maries, the road crested a sum-
mit and broke briefly into the open at the edge of a steep fall be-
fore disappearing in a few yards into the timber. From that one
spot you gazed out and down on a wilderness landscape trans-
formed by a lone human habitation. Your gaze traveled naturally
and easily from the log house and cluster of outbuildings up over
a tall grass meadow where horses grazed, and beyond the
meadow, upriver to where the timber and valley narrowed against
the mountains and the sky. It was a sublime allocation of space —
sky, mountains, and pasture — and through it all, traversing the
deep space of the landscape in a way that suggested its natural
function was mainly picturesque, flowed the river. The river
spilled down and across your field of vision, fast and shallow. The
sun glinted off the rocks and gravel as the river washed over them,
and along its banks and on an island formed where the waters di-
vided there grew stands of cottonwoods. Where the cottonwoods
grew most dense and tall, the river turned in a sharp arc — a fig-
ure of grace so exquisite it brought you to the edge of tears. Above
that stand of trees at that bend in the river was the meadow, cloud
shadows drifting across the grass in the breeze, and above the
meadow was the ranch. The most perfect ranch in all the world,
the house right there, as John Wayne once promised to the hero-
ine in *War of the Wildcats* he would build "at the bend in the river
where the cottonwoods grow."

My romantic opinion of Burger's place is hardly objective. I
never think of it without enjoyment, and yet my enjoyment often
comes with a considerable amount of irony. The ranch I fell in
love with is in the image of the slick, commercial American Eden
invented by photographers and artists in the nineteenth century,

an image popularized in fiction and film in the twentieth. Being there was a little like being permitted to enter a painting. Yet despite its artifice, I had the sense that in certain ways Burger's home was more familiar than my own. Perhaps for that reason it was inevitable that the ranch should instill in us a sense of wonder at our own good fortune, and each time we visited we felt as if we were crossing into a different realm.

Going to his impossibly remote ranch resembled an inward as well as an outward journey. The first time I drove to the place, I navigated with a rough set of instructions; the ranch that was gloriously visible from a long way off disappeared from view as I neared it, and the last mile of the approach was made mostly on faith. From deep within the timber, out of sight of the house and meadow, I passed through a gate, descended a winding and deeply rutted dirt lane, crossed a flimsy bridge over a rushing but nearly invisible creek, then drove through a long, cool, dark colonnade of cedar and hemlock that muffled the sound of the engine so that the car seemed almost to be coasting. When at last I broke into the open, the light and space were so intense that for a moment I shut my eyes against them. I was surrounded by sun and grass and the slopes of the mountains, an environment sharply distinct from the mundane woodland geography I'd left. It felt like a rite of passage, a kind of resurrection.

This sensation was caused in part by the almost monastic isolation of the ranch. It lay about ten miles upriver from St. Maries, accessible by car only from May through November. At that time, apart from Burger, only a single family lived along the road for the twelve miles from where it passed our house to where it bottomed, finally, after a series of precipitous switchbacks bulldozed along steep mountain walls, on the west bank of the St. Maries River. And that family scarcely needed a roadway at all. Their cabin lay more than a mile off the road, determinedly beyond the reach of electricity, telephone, or motor vehicle. They came as close to living off the land as anyone I'd ever seen, and when they needed supplies from town they usually walked.

The River Road was perpetually in decline. It was used only by occasional sightseers in summer or hunters in fall. Almost no one traveled the middle portions of the road during the other two seasons. In winter it was blocked by snow, in spring by mud. Once a year, in May or early June, depending on the timing of the thaw and subsequent dryout, the county ran a grader up from town to scrape the surface free of ruts and rocks, but other than that, they paid it no mind.

It's an enchanted feeling to possess a public road entirely. It's not at all the same thing as traveling on foot through roadless country. On any road, even one as little traveled as that one, you're never without the expectation of meeting traffic, and as a result you see things from a modern point of view. On any road, you always behave like a driver. It is not just freedom of movement that you gain, therefore, when a road is rendered impassable, but a different orientation to its space. It is like being given back something you were not aware you had lost in the first place, and you experience it through more primitive eyes.

Once we sledded down to Burger's gate, a downhill run of nearly four miles. I could not help but notice how sharpened my senses were to the landscape; I saw familiar sights as if for the first time, no longer cut off from them by sheets of glass. Another time Nancy skied the road to bring Burger, who was snowbound, a bottle of his favorite liqueur, blackberry brandy. The only thing she saw on the road the whole trip was the half-eaten carcass of a deer. You would usually interpret the sight of a dead deer on the roadside sympathetically but naturally. But stripped of the illusion that separates driver from landscape, the things of the environment can suddenly seem to enter into webs of personal meaning. The carcass, she said, had the distinct feel of a symbol; it was unnerving not because it was ugly or sorrowful but precisely because it seemed so full of hidden meaning.

Even in summer, we were among the few people who had reason to use the River Road, and often the tracks of our transit would remain visible for days afterward. It was strange to come upon signs of your own presence days or even weeks after you had made them. Tracks in the road were not anonymous and unsightly tracings with which you have no connection, but complex personal mementos. To spot them involved a type of adventure and intellectual pleasure, like deciphering puzzles.

Two miles downstream from Burger's ranch, the road left the river and began to climb, by way of a series of extended switch-backs and half loops, until it crested at the edge of Alder Creek Flats, on the nether reaches of the original Brede holdings, some five miles east of our cabin. The climb was steep and more or less constant. In five miles the road had to rise nearly a thousand feet, and by the time you drew abreast of Burger's place the road edged along the mountain wall three hundred feet above the river.

Despite the remoteness of his ranch, in the few years he lived in Idaho Burger acquired a host of friends. We met many of them on our visits. In this way our lives became briefly intertwined with a great variety of people. We became friends with railroad workers, loggers, schoolteachers from Yakima, and the grocery clerk in the St. Maries Safeway. Through Burger's agency we had dealings otherwise impossible. Brakemen for the Chicago, Milwaukee, and St. Paul invited us for a ride in the dead of winter upriver to Avery, near the Montana line; two years later, when we had decided to move, the grocery clerk supplied some much-needed cash by buying our truck.

Burger was especially adept at befriending people in law enforcement. For some reason he got along famously with attorneys and the police, and shortly after he moved onto the ranch a few lawyers and the St. Maries deputy sheriff became regular guests at his cabin. Once Burger's generosity toward his guests caused a scene of splendid irony. Among his regular visitors were several young couples, and they preferred marijuana to alcohol. Burger's solution as a host was to turn over a small area of his garden to growing pot. He had no interest in smoking it himself, and, as luck would have it, the plants thrived. By midsummer, Burger's stand of pot was several feet tall, crowding out the tomatoes and overshadowing the beans. Nobody could have mistaken those half-dozen plants for a serious cash crop, but there was no doubt he had more than enough marijuana to keep quite a few potheads happy and giggling.

The plants grew just off his deck, from where you could not fail to notice them. So it was a scene of dreamy bewilderment when one day the district attorney himself and Burger leaned out over the deck railing and gazed down while talking of deer hunting, politics, and the impending winter. The DA surely knew what he was looking at. Similarly, Burger knew the laws regarding the possession and growing of marijuana and the strain he might be placing on his guest. Yet so strong was the spell of Burger's household that the two men, one obliged to uphold the law and the other flouting it, could maintain the social harmony peculiar to those medieval courts where any guest was obliged to his host and any host, in turn, was obliged to honor a guest. The mood at Burger's place was like the Camelot described in the romance *Sir Gawain and the Green Knight:*

> And he the comeliest king, that the court holds,
> For all this far folk in their first age were still
> Happiest of mortal kind,
> King noblest famed of will;
> You would now go far to find
> So hardy a host on hill.

"The romance of the West may be misleading," says William Bevis, "but there is something special in the land, as anyone with a whole car and half a heart can see." Most of the time I lived in Idaho it was the other way around, with a whole heart and only half a car, but I still know what Bevis means. The landscape distorts all reason. You may well start out, as did swarms of painters and journalists in the early decades of the nineteenth century, with the ambition of journeying westward to record accurately what you see. But almost inevitably the scale of the land exceeds the capacity of your vision, and, like those artists, you lapse thoughtlessly into romance.

I would have liked to have stayed on forever, and for a time I believed I could — during the first few days I lived in Alder Creek I experienced the weird fantasy that I was staring at the very landscape I'd someday die in. But Ph.D.s in the humanities must follow job openings — on average, during the seventies, each year about seven or eight hundred new Ph.D.s in English competed for slightly less than half as many college teaching positions — and in 1979 an already difficult job market for English teachers reached a historic low. The year I earned my degree there were no jobs in my field in north Idaho — and few, for that matter, in the entire Northwest. I wrote seventy-eight letters of inquiry to universities, colleges, and community colleges in Idaho, Montana, Oregon, and Washington; sixty-five replied, each telling me they anticipated no openings. From the remaining thirteen schools I heard nothing. Perhaps they thought I was just kidding.

I had entered a world governed by iron Darwinian laws, something I had not imagined when I began my graduate studies, bewitched by literature. My search horizons broadened to take in remote possibilities like Keene, New Hampshire, and Bemidji, Minnesota. I felt powerless, caught up like a migratory grackle in a mysterious food chain. By the time I graduated in June, the measure of my slipping hopes was that I responded like one of Pavlov's dogs to an advertisement for a temporary job teaching composition in a town in Illinois called Normal. In my desperate state of mind, the name seemed slightly ominous, a warning that I'd better mend my ways. I wrote to express my interest; somewhere a wheel turned, and four days later the chair of the department called to offer me a title and a salary, good for one year only. The die was cast, and Nancy and I immediately set about dismantling the life we had so carefully built.

It all happened with dizzying speed, a frenzy of packing, selling, and simply abandoning. McPherson even offered me $50 for the chain saw. I accepted — our new yard in Normal held five small trees — but it seemed like a punishment. One of our last acts before moving was to give away all our uneaten food, a kind of appeasement to fate for our departure. We emptied the freezer and the cupboards, butchered and dressed eight chickens. My younger daughter, Laura, then three, watched the chickens being killed and cleaned with great interest; she'd never before seen this. For a long time afterward she was unusually silent, brooding. Then she began to cry. Tears streaming down her face, she blurted out a child's idea of leaving: "Do we have to cut the heads off my cats when we move too?"

As things turned out, instead of leaving, we became what the locals referred to as summer people. We returned to Alder Creek summer after summer through the early 1980s, packing the car and heading west a day or two after school let out, not bothering to put up a calendar until the arrival of the grasshoppers reminded us that summer was ending. None of us ever considered there was any other possible place to spend the summer, and for a few years it was easy to sustain the illusion that everything was as it had always been. In my imagination I was in Normal, Illinois — or, later, Atlanta — just for a few months until the end of the school term, when at last I could return to my real life. I subscribed to the St. Maries paper; I paid monthly stand-by rates for the telephone and electricity; the day when I made the three motel reservations for the trip westward was as important to my calendar as Christmas and birthdays. But it was the death of Frank Burger in 1986, more than anything else, that convinced me beyond any doubt that a season of my life had closed.

In the first years we knew Burger he was already suffering the effects of the diseases that would one day overcome him — his shortness of breath, his blue-gray fingers, his hacking cough that meant his lungs were filling up with phlegm. What killed him finally was heart failure, a condition made progressively worse by his chronic emphysema and by a case of pneumonia he'd contracted after spending a rainy winter's day coaxing stubborn horses onto a trailer. He only partly recovered from the pneumonia, and he relied more and more on neighbors and on a constant supply of supplemental oxygen, which he obtained, to save a little money, in big green tanks bought from welding equipment suppliers at Fleet Parts. He rarely ventured outdoors. With the steady loss of his breath — it was a cruel insight into the history of the metaphor — went Burger's spirit. His mood was often gloomy, and more than once he said he wished that somebody would "just shoot me." At times he became belligerent and abusive. Four years after we had moved from Alder Creek, one of Burger's close friends wrote to tell me why she had recently left. "As much as I'd once cared for the old bastard," she wrote, "I have to admit that moving off that ranch and being rid of him is one of the greatest reliefs of my life. At least one thing I can say about the sad ending of our friendship is that I wrote an essay about it for English 101 and got an A."

The truth? I don't know. But it seems significant that in that woman's life — as I think in mine also — Burger had caused a turbulence that somehow only writing could remedy. The pneumonia was the beginning of two years of steady and crippling degeneration. At first he chose to stay in his house rather than move to town — "I'd rather stay put even if I have to fork out three hundred dollars a month to breathe," he said. But he grew ever more dependent on charity, and eventually Burger moved in with friends on the outskirts of Ellensburg, Washington, where his emphysema relentlessly consumed his lung capacity until one day he commanded — there is no other word for it — that his oxygen supply be shut down, and within minutes he was gone. He died early in January of 1986; it seemed fitting that death should have come so near the winter solstice.

That year my family and I again spent most of the summer in Alder Creek; we lingered until almost the last possible moment before returning east for school. For two months I immersed myself in woods excursions and frontier carpentry, but by early August I could no longer defer making a visit to the house in Ellensburg where Burger had spent his last days. It was a fine house in a new suburban development, located on the fringe of town next to an irrigation canal, with a couple of acres, a small fenced pasture, and a stable. I talked sadly with the women who had cared for Burger about the old days; we walked around the house and grounds and handled some of Burger's things — clothes, a saddle, bits and pieces of his oxygen apparatus, a rumpled western hat with a hole in the brim where once he'd swatted a belligerent steer on the horns. There wasn't much to look at — I remember feeling surprised at how little one left behind — but I still felt Burger's presence in intangible ways, like a shadow of something real.

There was no grave; his ashes had been scattered, at his request, "someplace on a mountain." We took inventory of the things in his room, and then I drove back to Alder Creek and on down the River Road to the place we still called Burger's ranch. I stopped at the edge of the bluff that overlooks the ranch, intending to say farewell. Ten years almost to the day had passed since that afternoon in August when Burger had stopped by our place to inquire about firewood, and in the weeks that led up to my visit I had played the occasion of my returning to Burger's old ranch over and over in my mind until the trip became a kind of formal pilgrimage. I wanted to burn the scene into my consciousness. I was prepared to make a speech, even if that meant talking only to the squirrels and the buck brush. I had expected to be melancholy; truth be told, I suppose I even looked forward to feeling it. I'd like to put another and more flattering coloring on my attitude, but if I remember clearly, I was expecting to feel what journalists these days call the "closure" that follows grief.

I was wrong about everything. It was the first time the sight of the ranch failed me. To my surprise, the scene was not especially emotional. As I looked down on Burger's house and the river that had so long figured at the core of my life, my feelings were scarcely even nostalgic. Instead, I sensed overwhelming detachment and disbelief. I stood on the bluff — "the point" we'd always called it from below as we gazed up from Burger's deck — and looked out over the ranch. Everything I saw looked artificial, unnaturally distant. Even the most familiar objects and spaces — the brown ribbed tin on the roof, the corral where Burger had kept his horses, the steps I'd built to lead up to his front door — all belonged to another time and place. I felt no kinship with that space or anything in it, and I could not imagine my body moving through it. It was another world, and I stared at it for a long time unable any longer to believe in it.

It was the first time I really understood what Saint Augustine meant when, in his *Confessions,* he declared that our past was forever off-limits. It's the kind of sentence that affords you pleasure to read again and again: "When we describe the past," Augustine writes, "it is not the reality of it we are drawing out of our memories, but only words based on impressions of moments that no longer exist." The ranch, like the past, existed in my imagination, but I had no access to it. Lacking evidence that I had lived what I remembered, much of what I thought I remembered suddenly and for all time assumed the strange and remote character of a dream.

Two days later, the summer over, we were on our way east. In the car were the few things we had taken to commemorate Frank Burger — a doll's log cabin he'd made to pass the time one long winter; a mawkish oil painting of a river, a mountain, and moonlight; a twelve-gauge shotgun, Winchester Model 1898; a copy of his will (there were wives and children, I discovered to my surprise, he'd never spoken of); and a large poster depicting a locomotive dangling halfway over the edge of a collapsed bridge above a bevy of desperate workers, captioned simply, "Oh shit." That was one of the years our daughters took along friends to our summer home, and the car was uncomfortably full: two adults, four children, enough luggage for an assault on a Himalayan peak, and the myriad supplies children require if they are to endure a day on the road. We drove through southwestern Wyoming and crossed into Colorado, the sun behind us beginning to throw long shadows off the hills and along the side of the car. Over our heads and all around was the West's famous big sky.

The vista was breathtaking. The most insistent feature of the western sky is its size. It is that size, its impossible vastness and remoteness, that moves people to celebrate it in songs and on license plates. It is a sweep of the heavens big enough to comprehend more than one kind of weather. Even the children, often cranky and belligerent after a day in a car, fell silent and became absorbed in watching the drama of space and light and shadow. We were transfixed. To the north and east stretched snowy patches of cumulus formations, while to the south and increasingly behind us, their edges backlighted and set glowing by the westering sun, towered a line of deep black thunderheads.

I had been distressed by Burger's death, upset in ways I had not anticipated and could not fathom. I felt shaken and rudderless.

Like a pilgrim, I was, I suppose, looking for a sign, and when you are in a mood like that it's probably inevitable that the world will provide what you want. Looking at those competing masses of clouds, I could not help but think less of the glories of nature or the vagaries of weather systems than of philosophies, of fundamental principles of creation. It wasn't a sky I was looking at; it was a drama between the forces of good and evil, a cosmic morality play. Perhaps the Manichaeans had it right after all: the cosmos is hopelessly, helplessly split, and we are only bit players in God's grand psychomachia.

Rivaling the sky for moral intelligibility was the western landscape. The scene was not merely beautiful but sensibly, intelligently so. Its splendor was decisive, chromatic. Everywhere we looked there was emphatic definition and separation of colors: yellow light, brown land, blue sky. And those colors and shapes were all superlatives. The line, the sweep of an escarpment, was pure, unequivocal. The sky was not just blue but a blue of rare intensity, the fabled ultramarine of the gentian, of the unicorn's horn, of the arctic seas. Meanwhile, flooding the entire field of vision was a golden sheen, a light of such terrible saturation that it seemed to have both form and force. Like the sky and land, it was both a physical sensation and a metaphysical reality, this sunlight. Or, rather, not just sunlight but light itself — the *phos* of Plato and of Genesis, the *lux* of Paul and Dante. To traverse that landscape was next door to mysticism. Things were signs. Land and sky were hieratic languages, ethical propositions. Light and shadow, in turn, were generative forces. The world was a moral tapestry; it was a book, as proposed in the twelfth century by Hugh of St. Victor, "written by the finger of God."

There is a passage in Thomas Hardy's *The Woodlanders* in which a young girl passing through a newly painted swinging gate accidentally brushes against the surface and comes away wearing a smudge of white. It is a trivial incident of no importance, and for that reason it is the very sort of incident that gives novels the texture of real life. It is meaningful for readers because it is so fleeting. Elaine Scarry reads this incident as proof of Hardy's exquisite sense of the physical reality of his fictional creations. "So it is," she writes, "that a girl passes through a swinging gate. Soon she is through the gate. A minute later she is beyond the gate which, if she were to look back over her shoulder, would be invisible, eclipsed by an intervening lilac bush. The act is over, yet it is still with her: one might say to her not 'You have paint on your shoulder,' but instead, 'You have gate surface on your shoulder,' or instead, 'You have passing-through-the-gate on your shoulder.'"

I see Idaho in the same way. The years I lived in Alder Creek take up relatively little space in my chronology, but I still wear on my shoulder what one might call "having-lived-in-Idaho." That so much of it rubbed off results, I now think, from the ignorance I brought to nearly every situation. It is true that my inexperience of rural life forced me to seek out my neighbors in ways I might never otherwise have imagined, just as our collective poverty enforced mutual dependence more than it made us self-reliant. But there is another kind of ignorance that is closer to naiveté, a spiritual state in which one is helplessly open to novelty, like the primitivism we associate with childhood. This ignorance was in my case purely a matter of luck, the consequence of being a thirty-year-old schoolboy turned loose in a western environment that was in some ways more cinematic than actual.

For years after we moved away from Alder Creek, Nancy and I now and then made a phone call to the empty house. One of us dialed and listened to the sequence of rings, and then the other listened. We let that distant phone ring ten, maybe a dozen times, and then we hung up.